STRESSED OUT!

SOLUTIONS TO HELP YOUR CHILD MANAGE AND OVERCOME STRESS

D1509131

**MARY ANNE RICHEY AND
JAMES W. FORGAN, PH.D.**

PRUFROCK PRESS INC.
WACO, TEXAS

STRESSED OUT!

DEDICATION

Mary Anne dedicates this book to her two newest grandchildren, Cole and Molly—wonderful additions to our family—and to her husband, Bill, the consummate proofreader.

Jim dedicates this book to the team of dedicated dads from the Christ in the Rockies father-son experience.

Library of Congress catalog information
currently on file with the publisher.

Copyright ©2017, Prufrock Press Inc.

Edited by Katy McDowall

Layout design by Raquel Trevino

ISBN-13: 978-1-61821-619-9

Prufrock Press Inc.
P.O. Box 8813
Waco, TX 76714-8813
Phone: (800) 998-2208
Fax: (800) 240-0333
http://www.prufrock.com

TABLE OF CONTENTS

ACKNOWLEDGEMENTS

Projects like this require the work of many individuals and we'd like to thank Katy McDowall, our editor at Prufrock Press, for her expertise; Jodi MacNeal for her knowledge; Emily Forgan for her research; Nicole Bagge, LMHC, for her contribution on what to expect when consulting a therapist; and our spouses for their loving support.

Introduction

Stress is on your radar. A child that you deeply care about is in, or causing, a stressful situation. You have so many unanswered questions. Perhaps you've asked yourself, "Is my child normal? Is this stress, anxiety, or both? Should I seek professional help? Am I contributing to my child's stress? Will my attempt to help make the stress worse?" You desire to do whatever you can to help your child—perhaps even to the degree where you wish you could trade places with your child or somehow just take the stress away. We understand. We get it. We're parents and professionals who help families deal with stress. In this book, we will teach you how to help your child deal with stress because stressors can occur anywhere, and, simply put, stress is not going away. To the degree that we can within a book, we want to help you raise stress-resistant kids in a stressful world. Because we've parented four kids of our own, we know when your child stresses you do, too. Stress affects the entire family.

Each chapter is filled with easy-to-use techniques, activities, role-plays, conversation starters, and children's books that can help your child learn to manage his or her own stress. There is not one magical tool for creating stress-resistant kids, but rather you need a variety of tried-and-true practices that can be applied depending on the situation. For example, if your child is anxious about a test, she may need to apply mindfulness or deep breathing. On the other hand, if your family experienced the death of a loved one, journaling or coloring may be more appropriate. We've provided you the best practices for helping your child in a variety of situations.

This book is organized into three sections to teach you about principles of stress, where and when stress can occur, and many reliable stress busters. In Section I, you'll learn how some stress may help your child excel while other stress may hold your child back. We'll introduce the concept that all stress is not bad and that there is eustress (good stress) and distress (bad stress). You'll learn signs of negative stress and anxiety. In Chapter 5, you'll learn 22 proactive ideas for helping your child minimize the impact of stress.

Section II contains solutions for the situations where stress occurs: in the school, community, and family. You'll learn what to do if your child's stress includes school refusal, bullying, and test anxiety. In the community chapter, you'll learn how to protect your child from everyday stress, stress from world events, and even the stress of visiting a doctor or dentist. The family chapter contains activities to help you deal with the stress families experience when parents divorce, a loved one (including a pet) dies, a baby is born, or when your child moves.

Section III is all about sharing with you the best stress-busting strategies. You'll have proactive techniques to address stress. We'll cover topics including mindfulness, meditation, faith, and how to help shape your child's mindset and develop the ability to bounce back from stress.

As you read, you'll notice that sometimes we will refer to the child as he and other times as she. Regardless of the pronoun used, we are referring to your child, so simply substitute your child's name for the pronoun. We wrote this book to help you, and we wish you the best. Consider connecting with our community by liking our Facebook page, Raising Boys and Girls with ADHD (https://www.facebook.com/ RaisingBoysWithADHD).

Principles of Stress

CHAPTER 1

Put Stress on Your Parenting Agenda

The greatest weapon against stress is our ability to choose one thought over another.

—William James

KEY POINT: Stress can be a positive, motivating factor in your child's life, or it can make life miserable and interfere with functioning.

THINKING POINT: Am I modeling positive ways of handling stress in my own life?

Stress. It is a constant in today's society. Whereas some level of stress can keep us motivated and engaged, too much can overwhelm and exhaust us. If you are reading this book, you know stress is not exclusive to adults. Negative signs of stress are becoming increasingly common in children today, as society has become more hyperconnected and its demands have become more frenetic.

Some experts have called this era of stress the "terrible toos" (Chandler, 1998):

- O too many demands on parents' time, which reduce valuable parent-child interactions;
- O too much pressure to perform in school on testing and organized activities; and

○ too little time to relax, daydream, and play—often considered the "work" of childhood (p. 65).

As both parents and school psychologists, we see the manifestations of harmful stress around us on a daily basis. When you are stressed to the max, your child will often feel the secondary effects, as you have less tolerance, may seem preoccupied, or are generally overwhelmed and lack control of your life. When your child is stressed and anxious, you may feel it and see it in your child's behaviors, or he or she may suffer silently. Consider these stressed out children:

THREE-YEAR-OLD JACOBI, an adored only child, started hitting others and being defiant after his younger brother was born. Of course, some of his obstinacy could be attributed to his developmental stage, but it came on so quickly and coincided with his brother's birth that his parents felt something else was going on. After brushing up on the types of events that could produce stress in young children, his parents felt he was stressed from feeling displaced from his important position in the family. Jacobi wasn't aware of this emotion, and his language was not sufficiently developed to allow him to put words to his feelings.

TEN-YEAR-OLD ELLA had become very moody and withdrawn. Her parents were aware she often seemed unhappy when they picked her up from school, and she was reluctant to go to birthday parties. She seemed to take more refuge in her art. Her parents noted her paintings contained fewer bright colors but wondered if she was just refining her artistic expression. When Ella's teacher contacted them about a bullying incident, they began to get a clearer picture of the nature of Ella's distress.

STAN, AGE 5, cried in the mornings when he realized it was a school day. He clung to his mother or father when he was supposed to be putting on his school clothes. Most school days, he would start crying and complaining of stomachaches but never on weekends or school holidays. A thorough medical examination by his pediatrician ruled out any physical reason for his stomachaches. Stan was experiencing separation anxiety.

All of these children are showing signs of unhealthy stress but in very different ways. The expressions of stress will be dependent on the child's age, developmental and cognitive level, physical health, coping skills, emotional intelligence, personality, resilience, and the presence of supportive adults. Table 1 describes some common ways stress can manifest depending on a child's age.

As you can see, increased emotion, sensitivity, and tears are just a few of the ways stress overload emerges in children. Changes in eating habits and sleep are also common warning signs that stress could be developing into a problem. Some stress and anxiety are inevitable, come with development, and can keep children safe from danger like fire or deep water. For example, young children "ages 4 through 6 years of age have anxiety about things that aren't based in reality, such as fears of monsters and ghosts" (KidsHealth, 2016, para. 5). Children ages 7 through 12 are able to project into the future and often have some worries about situations where they have no control, such as bad things happening to them or their family, world events, or natural disasters. Like most of us, it is not unusual for children to have some performance anxiety. When thinking about your child's behavior, you may have asked yourself, "Is this normal, or is my child experiencing high levels of stress that need to be addressed?"

Regardless of your answer, learning more about stress and anxiety is an important step in helping your child learn how to handle stress, which is a skill set that will be invaluable regardless of age.

TABLE 1
COMMON WAYS STRESS CAN PRESENT IN DIFFERENT AGE GROUPS

5–6 YEAR OLDS	8–12 YEAR OLDS
Regression to earlier stages	Excessive worry about issues like germs, dying, safety, intruders, etc.
Hypervigilance or extreme sensitivity about their environment	Refusal to perform in front of others
Refusal to separate from parents	Explosive anger
Excessive fear of monsters and imaginary things	Reluctance or refusal to go to school or new places
Frequent crying	Hurting themselves by biting or pinching
Aggression	Making self-injurious comments
Night terrors	Withdrawal
Difficulty with eating or sleeping	Lack of interest in activities
Fear of being alone	Nightmares, difficulty with sleep or eating
Extreme difficulty with change	Bedwetting
	Somatic complaints, like headaches or stomachaches

There are many things you, as a parent, can do to help your child, including:

- O perceiving challenges accurately,
- O developing effective solutions to events, and
- O keeping stress in perspective.

Your own responses to stress provide your child with the best examples of how to respond to changing situations and challenges. As we know, children often mirror parents' behaviors and attitudes. By example, are we teaching children that stress can steal the joy from our lives, or are we showing them that it is a natural part of life that can be met with responses that don't derail our lives?

Researchers Brooks and Goldstein, in their book *Raising Resilient Children: Fostering Strength, Hope, and Optimism in Your Child* (2001), showed that children who are resilient see themselves as problem solvers, have emotional intelligence, and can navigate the challenges life throws at them (p. 1). As we know, stress can be a positive, motivating factor in your child's life or it can make life miserable and interfere with functioning. Our goal is to help you mentor your child as he faces the daily challenges of life, so energy won't be sapped by indecision and worry but will be channeled into productive ways to handle what life brings.

RESOURCES

BOOKS

When Fuzzy Was Afraid of Big and Loud Things by Inger Maier (ages 2–4) depicts Fuzzy the sheep dealing with common fears.

When Lizzy Was Afraid of Trying New Things by Inger Maier (ages 2–4) features Fuzzy's little sister, Lizzy, who is afraid of making mistakes.

Sometimes I'm Scared by Jane Annunziata (ages 5–8) discusses common fears through children's eyes and how they can deal with them to get back to being kids again.

GAMES

Go Fish: Anchor Your Stress by Franklin Rubenstein (grades K–5) involves open-ended questions the child must answer before requesting a fish card.

Dr. Playwell's Worry-Less Game by Lawrence Shapiro (ages 6–12) features "Worry Monsters," which kids try to capture.

The Stress Management Game by Berthold Berg (ages 8 and up) features an anxious terrier and a cat in a board game and how they deal with common social stressors.

ACTIVITY
TALKING ABOUT FEELINGS

Get your child in touch with his feelings. If your child doesn't have an understanding of "feeling" words, there are many books that explain them, such as *There Are No Animals in This Book (Only Feelings)* by Chani Sanchez (ages 3–7) or *Theo's Mood: A Book of Feelings* by Maryann Cocca-Leffler (ages 4–7).

Once you feel like your child has an understanding of feelings, make sentence strips like the ones listed below. Put them into a hat. You and your child can take turns picking out a sentence strip and responding to the sentence. Use the responses to talk about what your child is feeling and how he can be proactive in dealing with the negative feelings.

Sentences can include:

O Things that make me sad are _____.

O Things that make me feel stressed are _____.

O Things that make me feel happy are _____.

O Things that make me feel disappointed are _____.

O Things that make me feel excited are _____.

CHAPTER 2

Stressed, Anxious, or Both?

Stress is the trash of modern life—we all generate it, but if you don't dispose of it properly, it will pile up and overtake your life.

—Danzae Pace

KEY POINTS: Stress can have positive or negative impacts, often dependent on how it is perceived and handled.

It is never easy to face the possibility that something is not quite the way it should be with your child, but excessive childhood fear and anxiety are not to be ignored.

THINKING POINT: Could my child's level of stress be excessive and concerning? Is so, should I consider seeking outside help? If so, who could guide me in finding the right professional to help my child?

To begin our discussion about stress, we should clarify what terms like *stress* and *anxiety* actually mean. Often they are used interchangeably, but stress and anxiety are actually different. Let's take a moment to understand what each one means.

STRESS

Many people immediately think of stress as a strain or tension, and many dictionaries have adopted that connotation. Merriam-Webster defines *stress* as, "A state of mental tension and worry caused by problems in your life." However, today some stress is considered to be a normal part of everyday life that can have positive and negative impacts. Stress that is excessive can result in a variety of problems and have an adverse effect on health. On the other hand, some stress can be positive and propel a person to perform to optimal levels.

The definition we would like to use is that *stress* is the body's response to the demands and pressures that are experienced each day, some of which may contain perceived threats. Stress can be thought of as anything that alters our homeostasis—it is something that can cause discomfort and often requires a response. If these demands exceed a person's ability to handle them and he or she has no support system in place, they can be threatening and have a negative impact. Ideally, people will learn to control stress in their environment rather than allowing it to control them.

THE IMPACT OF LONG-TERM STRESS

Mindful Schools (2013) shared a perfect example of how stress carried over time can became a significant problem—whereas stress that is experienced and released causes no problems. The example featured a psychologist's presentation on stress management. She held up a glass of water and asked the participants to guess the weight of the water in the glass. Then, she told them that the weight of water didn't matter, but what was important was the length of time it was held. She went on to explain that if she held the glass for a minute, it would not be a problem. If she held it for an hour, her arm would likely ache. If she held it for a day, her arm would likely feel paralyzed. Either way, the weight of the glass didn't change, but the longer it was held, the heavier it became. She continued:

The stresses and worries of life are like that glass of water. Think about them for a while and nothing happens. Think about them a bit longer and they begin to hurt. And if you think about them all day long, you will feel paralyzed—incapable of doing anything. (para. 3)

STRESSORS

Stressor **is the term used to define the stimulus or "thing" that causes a stress response.** These pressures can come from a variety of sources—family, peers, school assignments, teachers, afterschool activities, new situations, or health related concerns. Stressors can also be internal, including worry and fear. They can be minor, such as an unexpected school assignment, or major, such as the death of a loved one or a serious illness.

Obviously, there are stressors that are unfortunate and can alter a child's life forever. These include:

○ the death of a parent, sibling, grandparent, or other significant person;

○ parents' divorce—even though it may ultimately be beneficial for the family, it is very disruptive at that time;

○ serious injury or illness in child or family member;

○ ongoing school problems related to a learning disability or Attention Deficit/Hyperactivity Disorder (ADHD);

○ a natural disaster, such as a tornado or hurricane;

○ serious family financial problems that result in significant lifestyle changes;

○ exposure to violence in the home or community; or

○ excessively high parental expectations.

There is no way that these stressors can be considered positive, but with support, children can learn to cope with these negative stressors, make the best of them, and not have them completely derail their lives. *Resiliency* **is the term for the ability to cope with adversity or be knocked down by it and get back up, while maintaining our humanity.** Stanley I. Greenspan, M.D., (2002) said that children who are resilient "don't get lost in their sad, worried, or anxious feelings of the moment; they use the experience to find solutions" (p. 19). As you can imagine, resiliency is a critical quality for coping with stress and something we should all strive to foster in our children, and it is an important topic discussed in Chapter 9.

There are stressors that can be very positive but still require significant adjustment. These include:

O the birth of a sibling,

O moving to a new neighborhood,

O being promoted to the next grade,

O gaining a part in a performance or a spot on a special team, or

O moving to another developmental level (e.g., independence to go somewhere without an adult, such as riding a bike around the block or walking to a friend's house).

SIX-YEAR-OLD ANTHONY had been happy as a clam in his Midwest neighborhood, where he had many neighborhood friends and a school he loved. His family was excited to relocate to a new region of the country where they hoped there would be many new opportunities for all of them. Anthony immediately missed his friends and found his new school to be much more difficult than his old one. He became sad and essentially shut down in the classroom. His parents recognized his stress and made great efforts to have play dates with his new classmates, and they worked closely with the school to help Anthony catch up in his academics. Even with lots of help, it took Anthony almost a year to adjust to the changes in his environment. His parents were concerned but knew that helping Anthony to work through the challenges would only help him build resilience.

Even though situations may ultimately be very positive, adjustments to them can be very difficult and result in some negative stress. Any change, positive or negative, requires adjustment. For example, even though an only child may have wanted a sibling, being dislodged from the exalted position as the focus of parents' attention will produce some stress and possibly a temporary regression in behaviors as the child adjusts. Depending on the child's temperament and support available in the environment, the adjustment time will vary.

Many other situations can appear neutral on the surface but will be colored by an individual's history, perceptions, temperament, coping skills, and support system. To say it another way, the same event can impact people in different ways. Stressors that can be positive or negative based on a child's perspective, coping skills, and temperament include:

O peers,

O upcoming events,

O afterschool activities,

O school, and

O camp.

For example, upcoming events can be positive and exciting to some children and anxiety producing to others, especially those who don't like change. If a child has a positive history at school, he will likely be excited going to the next grade, expecting to do well. On the other hand, if a child lacks confidence in academic skills or is fearful of change, then he may be wary of the next grade. When he is promoted, he will likely be worried about his ability to do what is expected, which will only reinforce his opinion that he is stupid. Another example would be peer interaction, which is likely to be significantly more complex than when you were in school. If a child's history includes having lots of friends, knowing how to navigate social situations, and enjoying the give and take of friendship, she will happily rise to the challenges brought about daily by social interaction. If her history has been one of exclusion, bullying, and fumbling with conversation, social situations can produce negative stress.

INTERNAL AND EXTERNAL RESPONSES TO STRESS

Responses to stress can be external in that they can be measured by skin reactions, heartbeat, or other physical functions. Stress that is excessive can result in a variety of problems and have an adverse effect on health, such as creating stomach problems, migraines, heart palpitations, and panic attacks. The internal response can be fear, worry, depression, failure to be assertive, or procrastination.

ACTIVITY

IDENTIFYING SOURCES OF STRESS

Young children often need help to label feelings so they can talk about them and hopefully gain some perspective in the process. Frustration, disappointment, confusion, anger, and sadness are common feelings that children may mention when talking about stressful events. Young children may not have the vocabulary to know how to label their feelings. If you enter "How are you feeling?" in a search engine or look on Pinterest, many posters will come up which depict different feelings and their accompanying facial expressions. Having a visual like that often helps young children. There are also numerous children's books that help explain various feelings to young children.

For older children, there are more complex "feelings wheels," which can be found online or on Pinterest, which can be useful in helping children attach a label to their feelings.

Once your child can label feelings, help him identify sources of stress or at least where or when he has uncomfortable feelings. Then help him brainstorm one thing he can do to help himself feel better in the situation. Start with small, manageable steps.

CONVERSATION STARTER
WHEN STRESS STARTS TO SHOW

The most helpful thing you can do for your child is to let him know you are there to support him in handling changes that can result in better stress management. Perhaps your child may respond to your sharing information about your day and possibly discussing a stressful incident and how you handled it. By doing that, you would be normalizing the experience of stress and helping your child see there are solutions or ways to handle stress. For example:

PARENT: My boss came to my desk with a sales report I had given him a few days ago. He said I had made a big mistake that needed to be corrected within the next hour. I thought, "Oh no. How did I mess that up?" Then I said to myself, "Everyone makes mistakes. I don't have time to worry about that. I need to focus and fix the problem." I worked really hard and was proud to finish before the hour was up. I think feeling a little bit of pressure helped me do a great job the second time. Did anything that was frustrating happen to you today?

CHILD: I don't know. I don't even want to think about school today.

PARENT: I can understand that. It really helps me not to keep things that bother me bottled up inside but to talk about them with people I know love and support me. Sometimes, together we can come up with great ideas for solving problems, or sometimes when you talk about a problem out loud, you see a solution all by yourself. Will you be willing to talk to me if something bothers you at school?

CHILD: Yes, I guess so, but now let's play ball.

Although this interchange didn't achieve the desired results, at least you shared the ideas that problems often have solutions and that nobody is perfect. Also, you have opened lines of communication. Try again another day.

ANXIETY

Anxiety **is an unpleasant feeling of apprehension that alerts you to a potential threat.** The event may be real or only anticipated. It is often an overreaction to a situation or stress and a fear that "future events will have a negative outcome" (Huberty, 2013, p. 20). We may experience anxiety as fear, nervousness, self-doubt, or uneasiness. Anxiety is one of the most common emotions experienced by children. If it is short-lived and passes when the anxiety-producing event is over, your child may experience temporary discomfort but returns to equilibrium. For example, he or she may feel anxiety before a big game or a test or when having difficulty finding important papers. Anxiety can be a normal response to a situation when it provides the motivations and adrenaline to perform effectively. However, it becomes a concern when it negatively impacts a child's activities, becomes the standard or habitual way of responding to challenges, and is unremitting. Children with a high anxiety level are much more likely to see anticipated events as having a bad outcome.

Anxiety can masquerade as other types of disorders and may be difficult to diagnose. For example, "while some children exhibit anxiety by shrinking from situations or objects that trigger fears, some react with overwhelming need to break out of an uncomfortable situation. That behavior, which can be unmanageable, is often misread as anger or opposition" (Miller, 2013, para. 6).

CONVERSATION STARTER
MOVING TO A NEW NEIGHBORHOOD

"I don't see your big smile as often now as I used to. I wonder if you are still feeling happy."

If no response, explain a 10-point rating to your child and ask him to rate how happy he is on a scale of 1 to 10, with 10 being the happiest. Then, ask him to rate how happy he was in his old neighborhood. If that rating is higher, ask him what made him so happy, and try to make a plan to recreate some of that happiness in the new environment.

> ## CONVERSATION STARTER, *CONTINUED*
> ## MOVING TO A NEW NEIGHBORHOOD
>
> You might help him by trying to arrange play dates with children who seem compatible or introducing him to some of the interesting things in his new environs. Let him know that moving isn't easy for the adults either, and you are working on being happier about it, too. Check in occasionally to see how the plan is working and revise when necessary.

ANXIETY DISORDERS

When it is experienced regularly to a significant degree and interferes with functioning, anxiety can rise to the level of a diagnosable anxiety disorder. According to Chandsky (2014), "Anxiety continues to be the primary mental health problem facing children and teens today; the incidence according to some estimates is as high as 20 percent" (p. 5). Many more suffer from anxiety that impacts them but doesn't rise to the level of an anxiety disorder. There are many different types of anxiety disorders, the most common ones being generalized anxiety disorder, panic disorder, and social anxiety disorder.

HOW DO I KNOW WHEN MY CHILD'S STRESS IS GETTING TO BE TOO MUCH OR IS DEVELOPING INTO SOMETHING MORE CONCERNING (LIKE AN ANXIETY DISORDER)?

As a parent, we know your primary concern is whether or not you should be concerned about the level of distress that your child is experiencing. Look at the checklist below to gauge the severity of your child's problem.

Does your child:

O have frequent and ongoing physical complaints—like stomachaches or headaches—especially when given a difficult or nonpreferred task?

O break down in tears for no apparent reason?

○ refuse to join new activities?

○ engage in habits that could stem from nervousness, like nail biting or hair pulling?

○ have nightmares or significant difficulty sleeping?

○ appear overly concerned about what others, like teachers or parents, may think?

○ worry about health or safety issues, such as germs, intruders, or something bad happening to him- or herself or family members?

○ demonstrate excessive fearfulness?

○ engage in rituals or repetitive behavior like frequent hand washing or refusing to leave the house?

○ appear jumpy or ill at ease most of the time?

○ have difficulty managing emotions (e.g., uncontrollable crying or aggression)?

○ exhibit significant changes in eating habits (e.g., poor appetite, overeating, or binging)?

○ tend to withdraw from family and friends?

○ try to hurt herself or himself (e.g., by pinching, hitting, or cutting)?

○ voice any suicidal thoughts? (Yes, children as young as 5 can have these thoughts.)

Obviously, your level of concern will depend on how many, how often, and how much the symptoms listed above impact your child. Good questions to ask yourself are:

○ How much do these symptoms interfere with his life?

○ Are these related to any recent event?

○ How long have they been going on?

○ Do they appear to be getting worse or more frequent?

WHAT SHOULD BE MY NEXT STEP IF I FEEL MY CHILD IS SUFFERING WITH SIGNIFICANT ANXIETY?

By answering the questions listed above, you may have confirmed that negative stress and anxiety may be an issue for your child. It is never easy to face the possibility that something is not quite the way it should be with your child, but trust us, childhood fear and anxiety are not something to be ignored. If they are, oftentimes, the problems will become larger and larger and more difficult to handle.

When the strain and pressure reach a tipping point and become too much to handle, a child can be at risk of developing an anxiety disorder or other mental health issue. The scope of this book is to provide general information to you as parents on stress and manageable anxiety and how to help your child handle stressors as productively as possible. If your child's anxiety interferes with functioning and is severe, it is important to seek professional help. Many parents start with their pediatricians, some of whom have mental health therapists or psychologists on their office staffs. Anxiety disorders can be diagnosed by medical doctors, including psychiatrists, licensed mental health therapists, clinical psychologists, or neuropsychologists. For a proper diagnosis, information is often gathered from a variety of sources, including school and home through interviews or rating scales. Oftentimes, a trusted pediatrician or school guidance counselor can recommend professionals in your area who have a good track record of helping children with significant anxiety.

If you seek professional help, look for research-based treatment for anxiety, like cognitive-behavioral therapy (CBT), which seeks to challenge your child's erroneous thinking patterns and to replace them with more productive ways of looking at situations and solving problems. Another program is Coping Cat, a manual-based treatment program (Kendall & Hedtke, 2006). According to Beidas, Benjamin, Puleo, Edmunds, and Kendall (2010), the program is for children ages 7–13 "who meet criteria for generalized anxiety disorder (GAD), social phobia (SP), and/or separation anxiety disorder (SAD)" (p. 143). It involves helping children understand their anxiety and develop coping strategies. It includes a mnemonic "FEAR plan":

- ○ **F** for feeling frightened,
- ○ **E** for expecting bad things to happen,
- ○ **A** for attitudes and actions that can help, and
- ○ **R** for resists and rewards (p. 143).

We find that parents are sometimes reluctant to seek assistance from a therapist even when stress and anxiety are significantly interfering with their child's life because of their lack of familiarity with the therapeutic process. We asked Nicole Bagge, licensed child and family psychotherapist, to provide some guidelines for parents on how to choose a therapist and what to expect during the process.

HELPFUL TIPS ON THE THERAPEUTIC PROCESS FROM A LICENSED CHILD AND FAMILY PSYCHOTHERAPIST
NICOLE BAGGE

It can be a difficult realization that you need help with your child's anxiety and that it is time to seek professional help. It's okay to need help and very brave to ask for it. You probably have a lot of questions: Where do I start? How much will it cost? How do I find the right therapist? Maybe even, what do I tell people about my child having a therapist? My goals are to help you understand the process of finding the right fit in a therapist for your child and family, provide some expectations of the therapeutic process, and to also give some helpful tips.

WHERE TO START?

It is important to trust your gut feeling. As parents, we have feelings, instincts, and ideas about what feels right and wrong when it comes to the care of our children. Some helpful recommendations on therapists in your area can come from your child's pediatrician, school, your insurance company's provider list, and your trusted friends. Ask your fellow mommy friends! The saying, "it takes a village to raise kids" is really very true these days.

Once you have a recommended name or names, start calling. Do you connect over the phone? Be sure to ask questions. For example: *Do you work with kids experiencing anxiety? What approach do you use? Do you take insurance? What is your fee for service? How long is a session? How long will therapy last?*

Once you have your initial questions answered, do you have a good feeling (your gut feeling again) about scheduling your intake session? You may need to call a few therapists in order to feel comfortable and confident in scheduling your first session, and that is okay. The right fit is what is most important to build the strongest therapeutic relationship, which in turn fosters change and progress.

BE PREPARED

Once your initial appointment is set with the therapist, get prepared! You will probably either be e-mailed intake paperwork or asked to print it out from his or her website. Fill it out before the appointment so you can spend the entire session talking, rather than writing. It is helpful to have both parents present at the intake if possible. Create a list of the important information that you will want the therapist to know. A 50–60 minute session can go by very fast, so you'll want to use your time wisely and make sure you are able to help the therapist understand your child and family. Think about what you would like to see your child get help with—your goals for therapy.

After the initial appointment, ask yourself some questions. Do you like the therapist? Do you feel your child will like them? Remember that the therapeutic relationship is the most important aspect when finding the right fit.

Then, it is time to schedule your child's first meeting. Talk with your child about the appointment positively, highlighting what the therapist is like and what he or she can expect. The first session is for relationship building and assessment. For young children, that could include playing games, drawing, or using putty or other manipulatives, along with talking. The therapist's goal is to begin building trust with your child and helping him or her feel comfortable within the therapeutic process.

THE THERAPEUTIC PROCESS

It is important for you to understand your child's anxiety. The therapist should recommend articles, books, and helpful websites to educate you. CBT is a scientifically proven approach that many therapists use because it effectively treats anxiety disorders. CBT will teach your child (and you) strategies and skills to help reduce anxiety. Kids are given the safe opportunity to act out, play out, role-play, and express situations with different modalities (art, play, drama) that are anxiety provoking and learn new ways to think about their anxiety as well as manage the stress. Your child will learn new coping skills that will include relaxation, muscle techniques, and breathing strategies. Your child will learn to identify and replace his negative thoughts and behaviors with positive ones.

It is important to practice the strategies or "homework" your therapist recommends outside of therapy in order to reinforce the coping strategies, which result in lessening your child's anxiety. It is up to you as to whether you want to share with others that your child is receiving therapy. Regardless, it is important to share strategies and insights with people who work with your child often, such as teachers, tutors, and relatives, so everyone can approach the issues related to stress in a consistent manner.

The length of therapy depends on a few factors, such as motivation, practicing strategies and tools, and the severity of anxiety. The more motivated your child feels, the more likely she will practice the strategies and utilize the tools in real time. CBT can be as short as 12 weeks but as long as one year. Medication can also be used in conjunction with CBT but is not always.

HELPING YOUR CHILD

A successful therapeutic experience is one in which your therapist works with you and your child to foster progress at home and in school so the child's caregivers and teacher(s) can best support your child.

Helping your child understand anxiety and feel better is a process. Your role is to acknowledge the anxiety in a supportive and nonjudgmental way. Talk with your child about the symptoms and how they affect him throughout the day. Share some of your stresses with your child and how you have been able to cope and overcome them. With the right therapist, your child and your family can overcome anxiety.

CONVERSATION STARTER
GAUGING YOUR CHILD'S STRESS LEVEL

To gauge your child's stress level, work with your child to make two separate lists—one of your activities and one of your child's activities. Then, rate the happiness or stress factor of each activity (whichever label you think will be most appealing to your child) from 1 to 10, with 1 being the lowest or worst rating and 10 being the highest or best rating.

If you choose the happiness category, a higher number would indicate the activity brings much happiness. Conversely, if you choose the stress category, a higher number would show that the activity is very stressful.

If your child is willing to honestly participate, the activity could give you insight into your child and the satisfaction he or she feels with life.

RESOURCES

How Are You Peeling? by Saxton Freymann and Joost Elffers (ages 4–8) features fruits and vegetables with various expressions to spark discussions of feelings for young children.

The Way I Feel by Janan Cain (ages 3–8) helps children understand various emotions.

I'm Frustrated (Dealing With Feelings) by Elizabeth Crary (ages 3–8) depicts situations that require coping skills and allows readers to choose their own endings.

Feelings by Aliki (ages 4–8) features many visuals of different emotions.

Max Archer, Kid Detective: The Case of the Recurring Stomachaches by Howard J. Bennett (ages 7–9) is written by a pediatrician.

What to Do When You Worry Too Much: A Kid's Guide to Overcoming Anxiety by Dawn Huebner (ages 6–12) is an interactive self-help book that uses CBT techniques.

Woe Is Me: The Wild Adventures of Woe the Worried by Matt Casper (ages 7–12) is a chapter book and part of the Emotes series, which includes small characters that can be purchased separately (available at https://www.creativetherapystore.com).

My Book Full of Feelings: How to Control and React to the Size of Your Emotions: An Interactive Workbook for Parents, Professionals and Children by Amy V. Jaffe and Luci Gardner helps children identify the intensity of emotions and respond appropriately. It is reusable and includes a dry erase marker so you can add situations unique to your child.

How Do You Doodle? Drawing My Feelings and Emotions by Elise Gravel (ages 8–12) has activities to help children express their emotions.

My Feelings Activity Book by Abbie Schiller and Samantha Kurtzman-Counter (ages 3–9) is a fill-in-the-blank activity book that helps children identify feelings and learn how to change them.

CHAPTER 3

Helpful Versus Harmful Stress

As long as it's not too stressful, we can build stronger brain function. If we have stronger brain function we'll be happier, we'll be less anxious, less depressed and we'll be smarter.
—Ian Robertson

KEY POINT: Your child may experience eustress, distress, or toxic stress.

THINKING POINT: Does my child mostly experience eustress, distress, or toxic stress?

The ways individual children respond to stress are as varied as the different types of stress they experience. If you are the parent of a hypersensitive child, you know the work involved in supporting and helping him or her learn the most effective ways of dealing with stress. If you are in that situation, it is hard to imagine stress can be positive.

WHAT CAUSES DIFFERENCES IN RESPONSES TO STRESS?

You may have heard the myth that response to stress is genetic, but it's not completely true. Some children are more high-strung than others, but genetics do not account for all variability in the way a person experiences stress. The time of day, overall health of the child, the type of day it has been, the people around him, and emotional reserves can all impact the response. Parents all know to tiptoe around children who are tired or hungry, so we could expect their capacity for handling stress to be diminished during those times.

Physical and environmental issues aside, when thinking about everyday events, the child's perception of the situation and her ability to handle it often determine the response. Some children are such perfectionists that making errors on tests produces negative stress, whereas other children are not bothered and hardly seem to notice. When you think about it, your child responds to small amounts of stress each day to do things such as complete homework, study for a test, practice for a piano recital, or step up to bat in front of bleachers full of spectators. How she perceives those situations will impact how she responds and how much stress she experiences.

STRESS AND THE BRAIN

Imagine yourself the last time you were really stressed. A stressful incident makes your heart pound, which pushes blood to your muscles and other vital organs. Your heart rate and blood pressure skyrocket. Your breathing quickens, and muscles tense. The "fight-or-flight" response may have kicked in as a survival mechanism for dealing with stress. Once the stressor went away, you probably felt somewhat physically or emotionally drained.

Now visualize how your brain worked during the stressful experience. You've seen brains images. Imagine how amazing it would be if you could peer inside your own brain. You'd see an amazing complex network of fibers that helps you deal with stress. When you encounter stress, your eyes and ears send information to your *amygdala* (pronounced a-mig-duh-la). This is the area of the brain that contributes to emotional processing. You'd see the amygdala sending a signal to your *hypothalamus*. This is the traffic control center of your brain.

The hypothalamus communicates with your body to help regulate breathing, heartbeat, and blood pressure. When you're stressed, your body's nervous system triggers the fight-or-flight response and increases your adrenaline. This provides you with an energy burst to respond to the stressor. Your heart beats faster, your pulse goes up, and you breathe more rapidly. Your sight, hearing, and other senses can become keener. If your brain continues to perceive the stressor as dangerous, your adrenal glands release the hormone cortisol. This keeps you on high alert. After the stress has passed, your nervous system calms your body down, and whew, you're glad it's over.

Does this sound like a positive experience? Media outlets such as *The New York Times* (Reynolds, 2016) have reported positive stress increases alertness, short-term strength, oxygen to the brain, ability to focus, faster and deeper breathing, sense of smell, and productive mental alertness. Is there really such a thing as positive stress for children?

POSITIVE AND NEGATIVE STRESS

Simply put, your child will experience positive or negative stress depending on how he or she perceives a situation. If he perceives the situation as positive or not a big deal, then the demands placed on him by the activity will not bother him. Or, if he has what Carol Dweck of Stanford University terms a *growth mindset*, he will not see the event as a reflection of his intelligence but as an event that is an opportunity to learn and grow.

SEVEN-YEAR-OLD SCOTTY awoke for his big day in the lead role of his school's musical. While he had butterflies in his stomach, Scotty knew his hours of practice prepared him so the stress he felt created excitement. Scotty was ready for the show and motivated to do his best. He was worried he might forget a line but knew that if he did, it was not the end of the world.

On the other hand, if your child perceives a situation as very difficult and feels incapable of meeting the demands, negative stress will likely occur.

EIGHT-YEAR-OLD EMMA was invited to a friend's birthday party. Upon arrival, she realized that out of 22 guests she knew only the girl having the party. Right away, Emma perceived the situation as negative and worried that she wouldn't have anyone to talk to and would look like an oddball. It would only serve to reinforce her self-image as an outsider and someone with no friends. She clung by her mom and did not want to go with the group.

Emma's stress is real, high, and interfering with her functioning.

EUSTRESS VERSUS DISTRESS

Positive stress is called *eustress* (pronounced You-stress) whereas negative stress is termed *distress*. The possible outcomes of the two types are compared in Table 2. The terminology may not be important to many parents, but we have included a brief discussion in case you are interested. As you can see from the chart, there can be more negative outcomes to stress than positive ones, so helping your child manage stress productively is critical.

Eustress. *Eustress* means good stress. That would be just the right amount and type of stress that propels a child forward with motivation and energy to accomplish a task. When you think about it, a young child

TABLE 2
EUSTRESS VERSUS DISTRESS

POSITIVE STRESS (EUSTRESS)	NEGATIVE STRESS (DISTRESS)
Improves performance	Decreases performance
Is short lived	Is more long lasting
Is infrequent	Causes excessive anxiety or concern
Focuses energy	Contributes to fatigue
Provides motivation toward goals	Contributes to depression
May accomplish tasks more efficiently	Contributes to high blood pressure
May give short-term memory boost	May create short-term memory loss
May help to fortify the immune system	Weakens the immune system
Is perceived as within our coping abilities	Is perceived as outside of our coping abilities
Feels exciting	Feels unpleasant

moving from one developmental level to the next experiences stress. Remember your toddler learning to walk—it took great effort and practice to finally master that challenge and move to the next level. At that point, most toddlers have lots of support in the form of a cheering gallery and lots of determination. Eustress is short-lived and tolerable.

Distress. When the challenges facing your child overwhelm the available coping skills, stress becomes excessive and turns into *distress*. Ongoing, chronic stress will leave your child feeling exhausted. Over time, your child's day-to-day performance will likely decrease because there is no time to regroup and return to equilibrium before another challenge presents itself. Your child (and you) may need a relaxing and stress-free vacation!

TOM'S 7-YEAR-OLD SON, CONNOR, had natural talent at baseball but he worried every time he got up to bat that he would strike out. Tom discussed how even the major league ball players often strike out, and some of the greatest hitters had more strikeouts than home runs. Connor heard this rational thinking, but it did not sink in, and Connor was still stressed. Here's what Tom told Connor to help him overcome his stress:

TOM: You know how you stress about striking out?

CONNOR: Yes.

TOM: Well, what helps a lot of players is tons of practice. See, the more you practice the easier it becomes to read the ball and know when to swing or hold. Do you think you practice enough?

CONNOR: I practice.

TOM: Is it enough?

CONNOR: It's probably not as much as I should.

TOM: Right, if you really want to be a good player, start practicing during your free time. You'll become much better and worry less about striking out. You can practice with the pitching machine in the yard or we can go to the batting cages. It's kind of like school because when you practice your spelling words for the test, you get a 100. You can do the same thing for batting.

CONNOR: But school is easier for me. Hitting is really hard. I don't like everyone staring at me when I'm up at bat. Plus, if I strike out, I'm embarrassed.

TOM: I understand. In baseball, your body will follow your mind. If you focus too much on not striking out, you body finds a way to strike out. If your mind sees the pitch and watches the ball, your body will give you a hit. In other words, keep viewing yourself as what you want to become: a great hitter.

CONNOR: Cool. I think that would help.

CONVERSATION STARTER

PERFORMANCE-RELATED STRESS

Sometimes we feel stress when we have to do things in front of other people. Some people don't like to read aloud, others don't like to sing, and some people won't try anything new if people will be watching them. In talking about stress to your child, you might ask some of the following questions: How do you handle it when other people watch you? What do you tell yourself in your mind? Does knowing others are watching you give you energy to prepare so you do it well?

TOXIC STRESS

There is a rare form of stress that occurs at an extreme level called *toxic stress*. It's unlikely your child is experiencing this, but it's worth a brief discussion. The Center on the Developing Child at Harvard University (2016) defined it as, "prolonged activation of stress response systems in the absence of protective relationships" (para. 1). Toxic stress is so severe that it can disrupt brain development during a child's early development. It occurs when a child experiences chronic abuse, neglect, prolonged exposure to violence, and caregiver substance abuse without any coping mechanisms. The effects of toxic stress are alarming and increase the likelihood of later physical and mental health problems. If your child is currently experiencing or already has experienced toxic stress (such as a child who was in multiple foster homes with no loving, supportive relationships), you must seek professional support because its effects do not disappear.

RESOURCES

Master of Mindfulness: How to Be Your Own Superhero in Times of Stress by Laurie Grossman (ages 5–12) provides strategies by kids, for kids to use in times of stress.

Puppy Mind by Andrew Jordan Nance (ages 3–7) features a young boy whose mind wanders, and he learns to control it through breathing and thought.

CHAPTER 4

Perception of Stressors

No matter how much we reassure our children, their sense of security will depend a great deal on how we as parents view the world.

—Stanley I. Greenspan

KEY POINT: Your child's mindset is one of the most important factors related to how he responds to a stressor.

THINKING POINT: How can I positively reframe a stressor so it empowers my child rather than scares him?

How a stressor is interpreted by the body depends on what kind of stress it is, how prepared your child is to meet it, and how your child views the stress. In other words, it's simply your child's mindset that affects how he perceives stress. How your child thinks, rates his own ability to handle stress, and how he approaches the specific stressor itself all determine if your child will experience the situation as positive or negative stress.

Consider two children as they approach a stressful situation.

AUSTIN, AGE 5, was scared of lizards. He was enjoying time with friends on the playground and they decided to go inside the plastic playhouse, but once inside, Austin saw a lizard on the wall. He immediately screamed, started to cry, pushed a friend out of the way, and ran to the building where his teacher was sitting. He was crying and could not be consoled, so she had to take him inside to the classroom and he did not return to recess. The next day, Austin would not go near the playhouse.

GAGE, ALSO 5, was also scared of lizards. It was the end of the school day, and he was waiting to be picked up in the car line with his teacher and other children as they sat on the ground outside of school. He was startled when a lizard ran across the ground next to him. Gage quickly said to himself, "It's okay, a lizard doesn't bite, and I'm bigger so he is scared of me." He watched the lizard disappear into the bushes.

The difference between Austin and Gage is that Gage took control and identified the stressor and then calmed his body using his inner voice. Austin simply reacted.

When your child is facing a stressor, consider these three questions:

- Can I change my child's environment?
- Can I change my child's expectations?
- Can I change or influence my child?

If you are like most parents, your first instinct may be to rescue your child from the stressor and remove your child from the environment. After all, it's uncomfortable to watch your child stress, and as parents, we've all rescued our kids at one time or another. Some parents may have their child changed to another class to avoid a bully, avoid theme parks that have characters in costumes, or remove a child from boys who play too rough. (A caveat is that any time your child's safety is in danger, immediately remove your child.)

However, small amounts of stress produce growth. As parents, we've all had times when we intervened to help alleviate a struggle that our child was going through. We only wanted to help. Beth Kaprive, a caring teacher and mom to Taylor, shared the following story.

I've always remembered an illustration that has been quite insightful. It is said that for a caterpillar to become a beautiful butterfly, it must go through some transitional stages. An important part of this includes the final stage of breaking out of the cocoon. When you actually observe this, the butterfly struggles a great deal to get out of the cocoon. If someone interferes with this process, wanting to help the butterfly so that it does not have to struggle so much, they will likely harm the butterfly. The butterfly needs the strength that it develops from the struggle to survive as a butterfly. Without the strength gained by the struggle, it will not have the strength to live and will prematurely die.

I know there were times when I intervened to help alleviate a struggle that Taylor was going through. I only wanted to help. When I read this illustration, it made me wonder if there were times when I should have not intervened or perhaps not intervened so quickly, in order for Taylor to develop the strength that can only come through a struggle. During times of stress, I so wanted the situation to become quickly resolved/fixed or better yet—go away. I know that I stepped in to try and make this happen. After hearing this, and certainly as Taylor is getting older, I have become much more conscious about when and when not to step in and try to help with a struggle that can potentially lead to Taylor's growth and strength. I am learning how to be at his side, but let him experience the full growing process, which may have begun as a struggle.

Most of the time, completely rescuing your child from the environment does not teach coping skills. Let's consider Austin and Gage and ask the question, "Can we change their environment and make it lizard-free?" We could keep the boys inside, but this would deprive them from outdoor experiences, so, in this situation, it's not realistic to change their environment.

Can you change your child's expectations? When a child is stressed, some parents reduce stress by changing what's expected from their child.

Stress is uncomfortable so parents say the words, "It's okay, honey, you don't have to do that." This removes the discomfort and changes what is expected of your child and may do a disservice to your child. Rather than lowering the bar to change expectations, empower your child by helping him gain control over the stressor. For example, 6-year-old Paula's grandma died, and after the funeral, the family went for ice cream. Now, Paula does not want to eat ice cream anymore because when the ice cream melts, "It dies like Grandma." Instead of never going for ice cream again and rescuing your child from the stress of thinking about Grandma, empower your child. Give a positive outlook by telling your child Grandma loved ice cream, and it would have made Grandma happy to know the family was talking about her while eating ice cream. Paula needs to learn that talking about a person who died keeps his or her memory alive, and it is important to cope with death.

It's difficult to change your child, but you can change your child's skill set to give him more coping tools. Take Gage, for example. He learned how to identify the lizard as a stressor and change the way he thought about it. Throughout this book you are learning tools to teach your child.

Continue to spend time strengthening family relationships because family support is a protective factor for handling stress. When family relationships are full of conflict, it contributes to your child handling stress poorly. Try to resist using screen time as a babysitter and instead interact more with your children by recounting family memories, playing games, and enjoying each other's company. The unity you create will ground your child in security and help him keep stress low.

RESOURCES

I Think, I Am!: Teaching Kids the Power of Affirmations by Louise Hay and Kristina Tracy (ages 3–7) helps children realize that their thoughts play a powerful role in what happens in their lives.

Don't Put Yourself Down in Circus Town: A Story About Self-Confidence by Frank J. Sileo (ages 6–10) highlights circus performers and their ringmaster as they learn to bounce back from mistakes and fear, learning to feel more confident in the process.

ACTIVITY

CREATING AND USING A STRESS BALL

Consider giving your child a stress ball, which is a small, squeezable item that your child uses when stressed. These and other stress relieving items are available to purchase in stores or you can create your own stress ball with your child. For this fun family project you will need the following:

☐ small balloons;

☐ flour, rice, beans, sand, or bird seed (one of the items);

☐ a small funnel; and

☐ a permanent marker.

The directions are simple. Blow up your balloon so it stretches out, and let it deflate. Place the funnel in the balloon's opening, and slowly pour in your filler item. Leave enough empty space at the top so you can tie the balloon. Use the permanent marker to decorate the balloon. Allow your child to use the stress balloon, and practice using the following role-play.

Imagine that anytime you are out of your child's sight your child stresses. Even in your own home, your child's typical response when she notices you are not within sight is to yell at the top of her lungs, "Mom, where are you?!" as you hear panic in her voice. You've explained that you'll never leave her for good, but she still constantly wants you by her side.

Try this: Explain to your daughter that Mom's thoughts are always with her even when Mom is not there. Point out that the stress ball has a picture of a face. It's Mom's face. Your daughter is to hold the stress ball and when she notices Mom is not there, she is not to yell. She should:

ACTIVITY: CREATING AND USING A STRESS BALL, *CONTINUED*

○ look at the stress ball and say to herself, "Mom will never leave me. She is coming back;"
○ squeeze the stress ball and silently count to 10;
○ wait for Mom, as she keeps squeezing the stress ball; and
○ when Mom returns, say to herself, "Good for me, I did it!"

Practice this several times as you continue to help empower your child to realize she has control over her thoughts and the stressor.

CHAPTER 5

Minimize Negative Stress

Hakuna matata.

—*The Lion King*

KEY POINT: Empower your child to understand he is in charge of the response to a situation and can often do things to make the situation better or engage in some activities that bring him back to equilibrium.

THINKING POINT: Which steps am I going to take to help my child handle stress more effectively?

If you have a good relationship with your child, are patient, and able to spend some time learning about stress, there are lots of things you can do to help your child acquire skills for handling stress. Obviously your child is ultimately the one who will have to actively manage the stress that comes her way, so one of your biggest challenges may be getting your child to be a willing partner in the process. (Of course, your assistance would not take the place of professional assistance if your child's stress level is negatively impacting your child in a significant way, but can complement it.)

Continue to educate yourself. By reading this book, you are taking a big step in helping your child. When it comes to childhood issues, often the more you know, the more assistance you can be.

Educate your child bit by bit. Of course, everything you do will be dependent on age and level of understanding. Some children as young as 3 or 4 can begin to label feelings and understand what causes them to feel certain ways. Books written specifically for a child's age can provide concrete, visual information on emotions, behaviors, and solutions to vexing problems. There are children's games that involve problem solving and handling conflicts and unsettling situations. Help your child understand that stress and anxiety are normal feelings that can be managed, sometimes to his advantage.

Don't forget the impact of modeling. Model how you handle stress on a daily basis. Even though you may not realize it, your child is always watching and observing you and will take cues on how to respond to overwhelming and vexing problems. Do you ignore the problem, cry and fret about it, or consciously decide the most proactive step to take in resolving it? Teach optimism by looking at positive ways to resolve situations rather than automatically going to the negative.

Be present for your child and really listen. Try to understand what he is saying and especially the intent or basis of what he is trying to communicate. If you can help him develop solutions to problems or encourage him to come up with solutions on his own, do so. If not, move on to a different subject. Don't dwell on the problem.

Be patient. If you are frustrated that you have explained something 10 times and your child still hasn't gotten it, think of how inadequate she must be feeling. Even though your child might not show it, she is likely to be much more frustrated with herself. In those cases, walk away and gather your composure rather than chastising her.

Be mindful of your child's developmental age. This is especially important with bright, highly verbal children. Just because you child may be highly verbal and able to communicate on some levels like a much older child does not mean he has the emotional development to go along with those strong verbal skills.

Empower your child to be a problem solver. Remember she is a child, so not all of her solutions will work out. Often, experience is an awesome teacher. Other times, she might need your help in learning how to break large problems down into smaller, more manageable chunks.

Teach self-discipline. Remind your child to stop and think about consequences before jumping into a situation. Many stressful peer conflicts could be avoided if the children involved were able to stop, consider the other person's perspective, and then decide the best course of action rather than blurting out the first thing that came to mind. Self-discipline can help children learn that immediate gratification is not always the best way to achieve a happy life.

Praise and reinforce effort more than the results. If your child has really tried on a test or project, then accept the results. What more can you realistically ask of him?

Lead with the positive. When Mary Anne's daughter was an adult, she told Mary Anne that she always felt pressured by Mary Anne because the focus was always what she missed on tests rather than what she got right. That was news to Mary Anne, as she only thought she was helping her daughter understand what she had missed.

Have realistic expectations. Not every child can be at the top of the class or have a perfect report card. If a child has average abilities, then average grades may be the best he can do.

Provide downtime. Make sure your child's schedule is not packed with too many things. Sufficient downtime is necessary to regroup and relax.

Find your child's passions. Find activities that help him get in touch with his creativity or completely engage his attention. As adults, we know that we can often totally relax and block out the stress of the day for a brief period while engaging in something we love.

Encourage independence. Try not to do things for your child that she can do for herself. Being independent helps a child develop confidence and good self-esteem.

Help your child understand that mistakes happen. Spilled milk, ruined sneakers, careless errors on tests, and hurtful words that are spoken before they are filtered are part of life. All parents want to teach their children and help them avoid hurtful situations, but remember that mistakes are a part of life. Discourage perfectionism.

Encourage your child to have a growth mindset. Children who view themselves as capable learners who get better with practice and hard work will fare better than those with a fixed mindset who believe intelligence is fixed and determines how much they can learn (Dweck, 2006).

Help your child use "positive self-talk." For example, rather than thinking something like, "I am too stupid to do this assignment," help her think about it differently and recall a time she tackled something hard and made progress on it. Rather than a negatively framed thought, she might think something like, "I did something like this before. I know I can do at least part of it."

Predictability and structure go a long way in helping a child manage stress. Be consistent, yet allow for reasonable flexibility, in your discipline. Have routines in place for chores—morning, mealtime, and evening—as much as possible.

Remember that children have "big" ears. It is only natural to want to discuss problems with other parents to gain perspective, but always make sure your child is not within earshot when discussing concerns. The old "self-fulfilling prophecy" can easily come into play. If you talk about your child as a "Nervous Nancy" when speaking to others, that role for your child will be reinforced.

Help your child learn proactive, healthy ways to handle stress. For example, using language to calm down, deep breathing, visualizing a serene place, ignoring rude comments and not taking them to heart, and making realistic choices about what can be accomplished are all proactive ways of handling stress. (See Chapters 9 and 10.)

Make sure you are providing healthy, nourishing meals, physical activity, and adequate sleep. Regular exercise also has a positive effect on reducing stress. Exercise releases endorphins that can help your child feel better. In addition, exercise helps improve blood flow to the brain, which can improve the way your child feels.

"Laughter is good medicine." Well, it is true. Dr. Lee Berk and colleagues (Berk, Fenton, Tan, Bittman, & Westengard, 2001) studied humor intervention with adult men who received treatments to suppress bad blood cells. These men watched one hour of humorous videos and had their blood tested before, during, and after watching humor. The study found that the laughter helped terminate certain bad cells up to 90 minutes after the intervention. It feels good to laugh and may reduce stress, so keep watching those funny YouTube videos. As children grow older and more confident in who they are, they may find that learning to laugh at themselves and their mistakes may take the edge off situations.

CONVERSATION STARTER
SHARING A FRUSTRATING DAY

Make sure your child can label feelings, such as *frustrated, happy, sad, angry*, etc. If you need help, see the lists of resources in Chapter 1, which introduce your child to an array of feelings or refine understanding of feelings.

Say: "Mommy had a frustrating day. Can I tell you what happened?" Wait for your child's response. Then, explain a situation in child-friendly language, such as:

I went to the store to buy a present for Daddy's birthday. I had to search and search for a clerk to help me. When one finally came, she had to go to the stockroom, which required more waiting. She came back with the sweater I wanted, but it was the wrong size, so she had to go back again. I paid for the sweater and ran out of the store, realizing I was going to be late to pick you up from school. I called our neighbor, Cynthia, who was happy to pick you up. When I got home, I looked at the receipt and realized the clerk had charged me the wrong price. Now I have to go back to the store. I just had to remind myself that sometimes things take much longer than you expect. If I had stayed calm about it and thought about something positive—like how happy I would be to see you when you got home from school—I might have enjoyed looking around the store while I waited, and I easily found a solution to getting you picked up from school. I think I suffered "silly stress" for no good reason. What do you think?

Then ask, "How was your day?" If no response, ask, "Which of these words would best describe your day—*happy, exciting, maddening, frustrating, lonely, boring*, or just *okay*?"

If you get a response, then ask for elaboration. If his day was less than positive, brainstorm how you and your child could do something to make the situation better.

Empower your child to understand how she is in charge of the response to a situation and can often do things to make the situation better or engage in some activities that bring her back to equilibrium.

RESOURCES

What to Do When Mistakes Make You Quake: A Kid's Guide to Accepting Imperfection by Claire A. B. Freeland and Jacqueline B. Toner (ages 6–12) aims to help children who are too hard on themselves.

Nobody's Perfect: A Story for Children About Perfectionism by Ellen Flanagan Burns (ages 8–12) is about a child who learns not to be so concerned about being the best.

Ten Turtles on Tuesday: A Story for Children About Obsessive-Compulsive Disorder by Ellen Flanagan Burns (ages 8–12) is about a child who learns to handle anxious thoughts and compulsions with the help of her family and her therapist.

Double-Dip Feelings: Stories to Help Children Understand Emotions (2nd ed.) by Barbara S. Cain (ages 4–8) helps children with the experience of having contrasting feelings at the same time.

Shy Spaghetti and Excited Eggs: A Kid's Menu of Feelings by Marc Nemiroff and Jane Annunziata (ages 4–8) helps children identify their emotions.

Understanding Myself: A Kid's Guide to Intense Emotions and Strong Feelings by Mary C. Lamia (ages 8–13) helps children with strategies for handling emotions.

ACTIVITY
THOUGHTS CAN CREATE REALITY

Talk through different scenarios with your child to help her see how thoughts and bad attitudes can color the outcome of situations and can impact her overall happiness. Here is a start for the activity. Encourage your child to add different negative thoughts balanced with positive ones.

NEGATIVE NELSON	POSITIVE POLLY
I can't do this.	I know I can do some of this.
This is the stupidest thing I have ever had to do.	I think I have done worse things.
This is way too hard.	I will start and then ask for help if I get stuck.
I will never finish.	This is long. I will take one part at a time, and before you know it, I will be finished.

Stress Is Everywhere

CHAPTER 6

Stress in School

High-stakes testing of students . . . has created the most stress-filled learning environment in this country's history.
—Laurie Schroeder

KEY POINT: School is a very different place today than it was years ago, with increased emphasis on testing, a more complex social milieu, and a much greater need for organization and well-developed executive functioning skills.

THINKING POINT: Which areas of school produce the most stress for my child? How can my child and I work together to develop strategies targeting this stress?

School is a very different place than it was even 10 years ago. Some children from chaotic home environments still see it as a place of comfort, but most children perceive at least some stress associated with school these days. In addition to the obvious emphasis on standardized testing for accountability purposes, there is much more monitoring of daily progress, increased academic standards introduced at earlier ages, a more complex social milieu, and a much greater need for organization. Teachers themselves are under pressure and their stress levels often filter down to their students.

After the family, school is the place where children spend the most time. Having them in an environment where they feel comfortable yet are energized to challenge themselves and learn new skills is important. When you stop and think about it, school can be a very complicated place with so many different demands. These include:

O navigating the physical space (e.g., learning their way around the school, including the location of classes, the cafeteria, the library, etc.);

O establishing relationships with the teacher(s) and staff;

O following the schedule;

O staying focused on assignments, meeting deadlines, having materials organized, and having the right items for each subject (these are executive functioning skills);

O understanding the requirements of the classroom (e.g., lining up, turning in papers, sharpening pencils, using computers and technology, following behavioral expectations, etc.);

O making friends;

O dealing with children who may be bullies;

O being independent when away from the family;

O learning the academic material;

O performing on tests and evaluations; and

O managing homework.

Difficulty in any one of the above areas can make school a stressful place. Beginning a new school year or adjusting to a new teacher can be stressful, especially to a child who doesn't do well with change. A mismatch between teacher and child can cause challenges. For example, some children function better in a highly structured classroom with a predictable routine and can't operate in an open, noisy classroom where things are more fluid. If a child has a learning disability, ADHD, or some other condition that may impact learning, the stress factor could be magnified. Of course, the major stressors experienced vary with age.

In preschool and kindergarten, the major challenges are:

O separating from parents or caregivers;

O learning and following the routine, such as sitting in circle time, walking in line, putting coats away, and handling supplies;

O polishing their rules of social engagement to make friends;

O becoming independent in eating and toileting;

○ refining fine motor skills, such as holding a pencil and developing writing and cutting skills;

○ developing impulse control—stopping and thinking before acting; and

○ acquiring pre-academic skills in reading, writing, and math—sometimes even before they are developmentally ready.

In addition to continuing to refine the skills above, major challenges for elementary school children are:

○ organizing materials and keeping up with deadlines;

○ completing and handing in homework;

○ learning to responsibly use the Internet and social media (dependent on parental permission);

○ navigating increasingly complex social communication among peers, often an issue with girls;

○ handling increasing exposure and awareness of national and international violence and tragedies, especially those that are school related; and

○ performing academically in the classroom on assignments, tests, and standardized testing.

WHAT TO DO

Stay connected with your child and talk to him daily about school. For most parents, saying "Tell me about your day," or "Did you have a good day?" yields little useful information. Instead, try to have conversations that don't lend themselves to "yes" or "no" answers or just a one-word response like "okay." Encourage him to tell you one thing that happened that bothered him, the best thing that happened to him, or one thing that happened that he didn't expect.

Practice good listening skills. When your child has a problem, try not to be judgmental. Don't brush it off, but don't dwell on it either. Keep in mind that what seems like a small problem to you may actually be a huge problem to your child. Remember her developmental and cognitive levels. Bright children often have reasoning ability beyond their years, but they still progress through the same developmental levels as other children. For example, a 5-year-old may have sophisticated verbal skills but self-control may be a work in progress, as it is for most 5-year-olds.

Observe your child's executive functioning skills. These include all the things necessary to get a job done—focus, organization, sticking with the task until finished, working memory, and self-control. Work with your child on shoring up any deficits you may notice.

When your child brings up problems, brainstorm solutions. You want to teach your child to view difficulties as opportunities to rethink situations and figure out ways to make them better. Don't feel like you have to jump in and solve every problem for him. When you do that, he will miss opportunities for growth. It can be very empowering for children to participate in resolving issues.

Maintain an open relationship with teachers. They are the ones who have "eyes" on the situation and can often provide a different perspective, especially about peer situations, than the one your child offered. If your child's view is radically different from the teacher's, remember that teachers can't always see everything. Some children who bother others are very covert in their behavior, so it may not always be obvious. The old saying "perception is reality" can apply here because often the way a child views a situation colors reality—even though she may not be interpreting it accurately. If you think your child is misinterpreting a situation involving a minor altercation, try to calmly help her see it in a different light. Often, asking her questions will cause her to think and reconsider. However, if the issue appears to involve bullying, it must be addressed immediately.

Make sure you have realistic expectations for your child. Not everyone can be an honor roll student. A child with average intelligence will likely make average grades.

Try to focus on the amount of effort your child puts in. If your child has done his or her best on a project or test, that is all you can expect.

Help your child develop a "growth mindset" as opposed to a "fixed mindset." As noted previously, Dweck (2006) has done extensive research on how a student's view of learning impacts the outcome. She found that students who perceive that they improve with hard work do better than those who feel that their success or failure depends on how smart they are. Guide your child in seeing that learning often involves risk taking.

Help your child understand that a test grade reflects how they did on that particular day in that circumstance. It is not a lifetime sentence. You want him to be able to say to himself, "I'm disappointed, but tomorrow is a new day."

Try to provide support when needed. If you realize your child doesn't have the skills to be successful in a subject, offer to help or, if you can afford it, hire a tutor. Sometimes a tutor can go a long way in preserving the parent-child relationship.

Be aware a mismatch can happen. In our practice and with our own children, we have occasionally seen that a mismatch between student and teacher is in and of itself stress producing. At these times, it is important to try to help the child navigate the situation. After all, school provides opportunities to learn lessons in how to get along with different types of people. After reasonable attempts to work out the situation, you may feel like a teacher is unwittingly contributing to an unhealthy stress level in your child. At these times, you may need to become a strong advocate for your child and explore the option of changing teachers. It is important not to color your child's view of his teacher with your own negative thoughts—keep those to yourself.

ACADEMIC PRESSURES

GENERAL SOURCES OF ACADEMIC STRESS

Although most schools are able to have children reading material at their reading level, many do not differentiate the curriculum in other academic areas, so your child may be expected to do work above (or below) his capability, especially in subjects like math and science. When children are perfectionists, they often find challenging assignments to be extremely frustrating and stress producing. They want to do everything correctly but cannot. Not only might they be embarrassed because their performance does not meet their expectations, but they may also be afraid for classmates to see how poorly they do.

Aside from the academic level of the work, organization of materials can be anxiety producing for students, especially for those with ADHD or learning disabilities. Often these students have executive functioning difficulties which impact their ability to keep up with their assignments, turn them in on time and at the proper place, and have materials needed for each class. If your child has difficulties in these areas, it is important to work with him or her to strengthen these skills. Our book, *The Impulsive, Disorganized Child: Solutions for Parenting Kids With Executive Functioning Difficulties*, addresses these deficits in detail.

POSITIVE CLASSROOM ENVIRONMENTS

Teachers who use students' strengths to boost their deficits and create a structured, nurturing environment are usually very positive for anxious children. These students often benefit from a classroom environment that promotes social and emotional learning and fosters peer relationships.

Often, teachers are experts at helping anxious children in the classroom, but others welcome ideas for reducing anxiety in the classroom. Specific strategies will depend on the nature of the problem. For example, if the child has poor fine motor skills and works slowly, less writing may be required until skills improve. If he is a poor reader, he shouldn't be called on to read aloud unless he volunteers. If he is a poor speller, perhaps the teacher can mark misspelled words in his writing, allow him to correct them, but not take off points in a composition.

Some general suggestions teachers might consider to help children who are feeling anxious include:

O providing written work in chunks so a child doesn't feel overwhelmed by long assignments;

O avoiding using red ink to mark errors;

O focusing on effort rather than results;

O allowing additional time when possible to eliminate the pressure of time;

O providing preferential seating for ease of monitoring the student and giving him easy access to the teacher for questions;

O maintaining close communication with parents;

O giving additional positive reinforcement when deserved;

O using the child's strengths to shore up weaknesses;

O working on the development of executive functioning skills if deficient, like beginning work on time, staying with the task until finished, self-monitoring his work to catch errors, staying organized, and using time efficiently;

○ trying to help the child become an integral part of the class and encouraging the development of friendships and acceptance; and

○ encouraging the use of relaxation strategies, such as breathing, visualizing himself in a calm place, or taking a mini-break.

TEST ANXIETY

Test anxiety has been found in students as young as 7 years old (Putwain, 2008) and is on the rise with the pressures of high-stakes testing. High levels of test anxiety often result in lower scores. That only stands to reason because we know the neural pathways don't function efficiently when hampered by significant stress levels. Memory can be one of the first areas to be affected.

However, moderate, controlled stress can often be helpful in "amping" up the brain to help students think more efficiently. The key is helping students develop their academic knowledge and skills to manage their stress so they can turn their anxiety into excitement to demonstrate what they know on tests rather than letting it deteriorate into mind-numbing fear that sabotages their performance.

The stress can come from within the student based on personality, problem-solving skills, confidence in ability, and academic skill level, as well as from outside the student in the classroom environment. When Mary Anne served as a school psychologist within a large school district, she observed that even the most competent teachers could not completely hide their own anxiety about testing from their students. If the school environment is full of stress, of course some of that is going to filter down to the student.

Casbarro (2016) identified three components of test anxiety, which include:

○ physiological, like nausea, headaches, heart palpitations, or shallow breathing;

○ emotional, like crying, shaking, panic, or sense of powerlessness; and

○ mental/cognitive, like inattention, memory loss, faulty logic or sense of failure (p. 1).

If changes are not made to reduce the number of assessments students are required to take in a given year, the current environment is one that we have to help our students learn to manage to the best of their ability. Parents can assist students in reducing test anxiety by providing:

O   reassurance that your love is not dependent on a test score and that perfection is not expected;

O   acceptance of scores as long as your child put forth his or her best effort—praise effort more than results;

O   realistic, attainable expectations—not every student can be an A or even a B student;

O   understanding that test anxiety may be very real to your student, so be available to listen, and avoid criticism and impatience—don't let your child see your own anxiety about her performance;

O   assistance in preparing for the test—understand what will be tested and take advantage of practice tests if offered, as students with anxiety often benefit from "overlearning" material so they can feel more confident about it;

O   study schedules—studying a subject 15–20 minutes a night over a period of time results in better recall than trying to cram everything in the night before;

O   assistance in understanding brain function—your child's brain can't function at maximum efficiency if derailed by significant anxiety, so learning some self-calming strategies (covered in more detail in later chapters) is in his best interest;

O   encouragement to ask questions in class if directions are unclear; and

O   provision of a structured home environment that has reasonable bedtimes, physical activity, and nutritious food.

To combat test anxiety, it is important for students to:

O   make sure to sit away from distractions, like a noisy air conditioner, a door, etc.;

O   stay positive and don't allow negative thoughts to take over;

O   know how much time they have and monitor time throughout the test;

○ try to stay calm and in control because that is how the brain functions best—though a moderate degree of being "amped up" can be helpful;

○ use relaxation techniques when necessary;

○ read directions carefully and ask for clarification when needed;

○ first do the questions that count the most and that they know the best;

○ refocus when necessary;

○ try to answer all questions if time permits;

○ read and consider all answer choices carefully on multiple choice questions; and

○ check work if time permits.

It is important to note that in some states parents are banding together to push back against standardized tests in the public schools, especially testing used to determine promotions or placement in remedial classes. Some of their positions include the concerns about the significant anxiety experienced by parents, teachers, and students; the expense of administration of the tests; delays in receiving constructive feedback from the tests; and the questionable reliability of some tests. These parents are petitioning for the right to have their children opt out of testing.

RESOURCES

Stickley Sticks to It!: A Frog's Guide to Getting Things Done by Brenda S. Miles (ages 4–8) shows children how to persevere until a job is finished.

Annie's Plan: Taking Charge of Schoolwork and Homework by Jeanne Kraus (ages 4–8) shows a girl establishing a plan to improve her organizational and study skills.

Sam and Gram and the First Day of School by Dianne Blomberg (ages 4–6) takes readers through a typical first day of school.

School Made Easier: A Kid's Guide to Study Strategies and Anxiety-Busting Tools by Wendy L. Moss and Robin Deluca-Acconi (ages 10–13) teaches students how to avoid being overwhelmed so they can reduce their anxiety and improve school-related skills.

RESISTANCE TO GO TO SCHOOL

It is estimated that 4.1%–4.7% of children aged 7–11 experience school refusal and separation anxiety (Bernstein, 2014). Based on research and our own experience, there are two peak times of incidences of school refusal. As you might expect, the first one is in kindergarten when a child is beginning school (ages 5–6) and the second one occurs during the middle years (ages 8–10).

In kindergarten, the anxiety is often related to separation anxiety and/or difficulty in adjusting to a new situation. These days, most children have attended preschool, but kindergarten is a big change in environment and often in the length of the school day. For many children, kindergarten represents the longest amount of time they have been away from their family or caregivers.

Middle elementary grades represent another bump in the incidence of school refusal because children's cognition has broadened to the point where they can think in terms of the future and are more cognizant of how they impact other people, how they are perceived by others, and can think about events that could happen in the future.

It is important to understand that school anxiety should not be viewed as a behavioral problem that the elementary-age child has control over. It is usually a physiological response from a brain, which feels threatened whether or not there is an actual threat.

School refusal should be addressed early and will usually require a collaborative effort. Often it is critical to involve your child's pediatrician to ensure there is not a physical basis for the problem. School staff, especially the teacher and support personnel available like a guidance counselor or school psychologist, would be important parts of the team. If the school refusal does not respond to behavioral interventions and parent-school interventions, an outside therapist may be needed.

WHAT CAUSES SCHOOL REFUSAL?

Sometimes it is precipitated by a desire to avoid a specific problem or event, like a bullying incident, altercation, test, or difficult schoolwork. It can be related to avoidance of a perceived threat, or in some rare cases, desire for additional attention. When you think about it, a child who refuses to attend school is getting more attention than the child who attends dutifully—just because of the nature of the problem. A review of the research and Mary Anne's experience in school settings shows that it often occurs following a weekend or a vacation. In some cases, it is related to generalized anxiety or depression. Often there is a family history of anxiety.

Common causes of school refusal include:

○ concern about separating from loved ones—sometimes children also worry about the safety of their parents or siblings while they are away from them;

○ difficulty adjusting to change, especially at the beginning of the school year or when there is a teacher change;

○ a teacher/student mismatch—some sensitive children cannot handle a teacher who raises his or her voice, or some disorganized children require a highly structured teacher;

○ lack of skill to meet academic demands;

○ peer issues, loneliness, or bullying;

○ overstimulation in the school environment or sensory issues, such as difficulty dealing with noise levels, wide open spaces, or being in close proximity to others;

○ boredom; and

○ mental health issues, such as anxiety, depression, bipolar disorder, or oppositional defiant disorder.

Parents rarely think about the school experience from a child's perspective, but adjusting to a new schedule, new teacher(s), and new classmates can be a daunting task. If this is the child's first year in a new school, another layer of adjustment has been added. One thing to keep in mind is how a child, especially a young child, views time. Although the length of a school day goes by in a flash for an adult, an anxious child can view it as an eternity.

SECOND-GRADER ELISSA was very bright and accelerated in her academics, especially math. She had a high energy level and loved to be busy. She worked quickly and often finished her work before her classmates. The downside was she occasionally made careless errors. Her teacher was very rigid and wouldn't allow Elissa to read or do other activities after finishing her work, preferring instead that Elissa spend her time checking her work.

In Elissa's mind, she had a hard enough time focusing on the work the first time, much less going over it a second time. Over time, she began to have serious resentment toward the teacher, not only for her rigidity, but also because she yelled constantly and created a very unhappy classroom atmosphere. Elissa began to hate school, and it became increasingly difficult for her mom to get her to school. Elissa would often balk and say she wasn't going. It was exhausting to get her in the car, but once Elissa got to school, she was able to get through the day.

Elissa's mom went in to school for a conference and also consulted a psychologist, who felt Elissa was developing school phobia. After much discussion, the school decided to move Elissa to a different class, where the teacher differentiated instruction, had a calm and orderly classroom, and encouraged children with praise and recognition. Although it took a while, Elissa's anxiety about school improved and she began to relax in a calmer environment.

WHAT TO DO WHEN YOUR CHILD DOESN'T WANT TO GO TO SCHOOL

Do everything you can to get your child in school. This is one of the most important pieces of advice because compulsory school attendance laws are in place in every state. Every time the child stays home from school, that behavior is reinforced. Mary Anne had the experience of carrying one of her young children to the car kicking and screaming because of reluctance to go to school, which was ultimately resolved by a classroom change. Every situation is different, but she believed that giving in would have only made it more difficult the next day. Believe it or not, schools are very accustomed to handling school refusal and can usually get the child to walk to the classroom after you have dropped him off. If your child does end up staying home one day, make sure it is just as much work or more work than school. The last thing you want is for a day off from school to seem like a break. If you can't get your child to school, it is imperative to seek professional help right away because it could be a forerunner of significant mental health issues.

Consult your pediatrician to rule out any physical reason for the anxiety. Some children have physical reactions, such as tantrums, headaches, stomachaches, or increased heart rates, while others show only emotional indicators like crying and sadness, but it is still important to have it checked out.

Establish a collaborative team at school. This should include the teacher, guidance counselor or school psychologist, and anyone at the school who may have a special relationship with your child. The team should try to determine specific reasons for the refusal and then develop interventions targeting those reasons. Research shows that cognitive behavioral therapy is effective but is often not available within the school setting and must be accessed privately. It is especially important to determine if there is any bullying or exclusion, either overt or covert, occurring in the classroom and address the issues involved.

Address academic factors. If your child is overwhelmed at school, work on organizational skills your child needs in the classroom and seek assistance from the teacher. If there are skill deficits, identify areas that might benefit from tutoring and see if the teacher can modify assignments until your child's anxiety comes under control. In cases of academic deficits, work with the school to rule out any underlying learning disability and see if additional tutoring is available.

Seek professional help. If your child does not respond to school-based interventions, seek professional help through a licensed mental health counselor or psychologist. As noted above, cognitive behavioral therapy has proven to be effective in many cases. Sometimes medication for anxiety is necessary, at least until the child can benefit from therapy. Addressing issues earlier rather than later is critical.

Teach your child about anxiety. Depending on your child's ability, help him or her understand the deceptive nature of the anxiety, the unpredictability of it, and then experiment with different strategies to help control it. The website Hey Sigmund: Where the Science of Psychology Meets the Art of Being Human has great strategies and information for parents and children available at: http://www.heysigmund.com/anxiety-in-kids.

Stick to a routine. Try to have a structured, calm routine for your child prior to leaving for school. Do your best to ensure your child is getting adequate sleep.

Find strategies that work for your child. Some small children with separation anxiety benefit from having a small picture of their family to keep in their desks, on a small key chain, or laminated to keep in their pocket.

BRANDON WAS A THIRD GRADER with strong academic skills. He liked his teacher and had friends in the classroom but showed little enthusiasm for school. Two months into the school year, Brandon arrived at school late looking very distressed. His mother told the office that she was having an increasingly difficult time getting Brandon to school. He begged and pleaded to stay home, saying his stomach hurt. The school psychologist and teacher conferenced with Brandon to determine if anything in the school environment was bothering him and found nothing. Incentives of his choosing were set up to reward on-time attendance, including the opportunities to read with kindergarteners and assist his teachers with jobs—both strong preferences for him. His mother implemented outside therapy because individual counseling at school was not available. His reluctance to come to school increased, and he would arrive at school later and later crying loudly and having difficulty getting his breath. Mrs. Hicks, his mother, reported that he was also reluctant to leave his room to go places with his family. At that point, a visit to a psychiatrist was recommended, and Brandon benefitted from medication.

CONVERSATION STARTER
WHEN SCHOOL-RELATED ISSUES POP UP

Ask: "You don't seem to be as enthusiastic about school this year. What is different about it?"

If no response, try being a little more specific: "How would you rate the kids in your class from 1 to 10?" If asking for ratings is successful, you might pursue that line of questioning about other areas, such as the difficulty level of the work, the schedule, the teacher, etc. If you suspect something specific, then ask about it. For example, "Are you missing (name of friend who was in last year's class)?"

If your child is generally unresponsive to questions, you might try comparing the current teacher to one you may have had as a child. Sometimes that can prompt some comments. The important thing is to be supportive of the teacher and the school until you have concrete evidence that would suggest concerns.

If your child has a problem with the teacher, remember there are always two sides to every story. Most principals do not like to move children during the year, so if there is a conflict, it will be important to help your child work through it rather than add fuel to the fire by taking the child's side and bashing the teacher.

If your child continues to be reluctant to discuss school, don't probe further at this time, but assure your child you are there to help him figure out how to make things better because you value education, want it to be a positive experience for him, and have a responsibility to see that he is in school.

RESOURCES

Oh No, School! by Hae-Kyung Chang (ages 4–7) is a story about a young girl who does not want to go to school but is encouraged by her mother to think differently about the things she doesn't like about school.

School Made Easier: A Kid's Guide to Study Strategies and Anxiety-Busting Tools by Wendy L. Moss and Robin Deluca-Acconi (ages 9–13) provides strategies to reduce school stress that are fun to learn and keep students from feeling overwhelmed.

SOCIAL PRESSURES

In addition to the academic pressures, peer issues can be a great source of stress. Social pressures in elementary school often include breakup of friendships, exclusions from group activities, or bullying. Sometimes a child experiences stress because he does not have the social skills necessary to navigate the increasingly complex social situations he is experiencing. If you feel social pressures are a source of stress for your child, put on your detective hat and conference with your child's teacher about the nature of the problem.

The root of the social problems in the school setting can be very complex, emanating from a variety of sources, including but not limited to:

O Delayed social skills in your child, including difficulty reading nonverbal behavior, following and participating in the give and take of conversation, or respecting personal space of others.

» **Solution:** Work with your child to develop missing skills through modeling them yourself, talking about them, and pointing out age-appropriate social skills in books or movies. Structured playdates with a compatible child can provide practice for new skills. If you feel the skills deficits are beyond your expertise, speech language pathologists, mental health therapists, school psychologists, or clinical psychologists work on social skill development.

O Off-putting behavior, including impulsivity—acting before thinking about the consequences; egocentricity—always wanting things his way; or limited interest in interacting with other children.

» **Solution:** Practice stopping and thinking about the consequences of actions. Some children benefit from visualizing a big red stop sign to cue them to stop and think before doing something. If your child is insistent on having her way, books and stories (see list of resources at the end of this section) often provide concrete examples of how tiresome this behavior is to others. If your child tends to be a loner, it is important to recognize that temperament but encourage friendships without being too pushy. Our experience has been that children who are without friends suffer in middle school, so try to be proactive in helping them seek out activities—like sports, music, or art—that enable them to make some connection with others.

○ Bullying, including exclusionary behavior, from a classmate.
　» **Solution:** Bullying needs to be taken seriously and addressed by the parent, teacher, and the school in a collaborative manner. StopBullying.gov (https://www.stopbullying.gov) is a governmental website that is a good resource. See the following section on cyberbullying, which is becoming a problem even for older elementary children.

○ Depression or social anxiety.
　» **Solution:** Seek professional help through a licensed mental health counselor, clinical psychologist, or psychiatrist.

CYBERBULLYING

Social issues have taken on a whole different level of complexity with the advent of social media. Children are using social media at younger and younger ages, and children in elementary school may be exposed to cyberbullying. Cyberbullying is defined as mean, threatening, or demeaning messages delivered over the Internet. Obviously, being publicly shamed is a huge source of stress and one that children may be very reluctant to disclose to others out of embarrassment, fear of retaliation, or guilt. If you do find out your child has been exposed to cyberbullying, it is important to try to see this type of harassment from a child's viewpoint. They can't put it in perspective like adults and have difficulty projecting what their life will be like 10 years from now. Every day in the life of a child can seem like an eternity and result in a frequent refrain of "My life is ruined."

How much privacy you allow your child on the Internet is a personal decision. It almost goes without saying that a child's judgment is still a work in progress. Based on our experience and the situations we have seen children get themselves into, we advise oversight—looking at what your kids are posting, knowing who their friends are, and checking on which websites they visit. Their impulsivity may not be fully reigned in, or they may not be perceptive enough to see through some Internet "come ons" or read between the lines in some conversations.

Many parents these days have to work so hard to provide for their families that they have little energy to oversee their children's friendships and use of social media. Even when parents try to be involved, their children are often so much more sophisticated in their use of technology that they can outwit their parents. However, this is one area you cannot ignore.

RESOURCES

Books

Nobody Likes Me, Everybody Hates Me: The Top 25 Friendship Problems and How to Solve Them by Michele Borba is a book for parents about teaching children friendship-building skills.

It's Mine! by Leo Lionni (ages 3–7) features three funny frogs who learn to share.

Sally Sore Loser: A Story About Winning and Losing by Frank J. Sileo (ages 4–8) is about helping a child learn to value having fun over winning and losing.

I Don't Know Why . . . I Guess I'm Shy: Taming Imaginary Fears by Barbara Cain (ages 4–8) shows children that being shy doesn't have to limit fun and friendships.

Boss No More by Estelle Meens (ages 4–8) depicts the results of always wanting to be in charge.

Toodles and Teeny: A Story About Friendship by Jill Neimark and Marcella Bakur Weiner (ages 4–8) features friendship in the making.

Friends Always by Tanja Wenisch (ages 4–8) shows the vacillation of children's friendships between fighting and making up.

Dealing With Bullies by Pam Scheunemann (ages 4–6) contains full glossy pictures appropriate for younger children.

Martha Doesn't Share! by Samantha Berger (ages 4–8) helps Martha learn that when you don't share, you play alone.

I'm Like You, You're Like Me: A Child's Book About Understanding and Celebrating Each Other by Cindy Gainer (ages 4–8) helps children discover differences.

Blue Cheese Breath and Stinky Feet: How to Deal with Bullies by Catherine DePino (ages 6–12) involves parents helping a student devise plans for dealing with a school bully.

Circle of Three: Enough Friendship to Go Around? by Elizabeth Brokamp (ages 8–12) features three girls who are best friends but have their ups and downs.

Games

How to Be a Bully . . . NOT! by Marcia Nass is a book and card game for young children that teaches what bullies do and how not to respond to it.

The Bullying Game by Berthold Berg (ages 8 and up) focuses on the victim, the bully, and the bystander, helping children understand a bully's motivation.

Stop Bullying Thumball is a 4-inch ball with 32 facets with questions or prompts about bullying.

WHEN MORE SUPPORT IS NEEDED IN THE CLASSROOM

If your child has a documented disability and shows a need for modifications in testing or classwork, a 504 accommodation plan or Exceptional Student Education (ESE) Individualized Education Plan (IEP) may be provided, which could include items like extended time, flexible setting, or math problems read aloud. Check with your school for more information long before these accommodations may be needed because it is often a cumbersome process.

If your child has 504 or ESE testing accommodations, ensure that they are in place at the school. If your child is 8 years old or older, make sure your child understands what they are.

ANTOINE AND HIS TWIN SISTER were successful in their pre-kindergarten class, and his teacher noted no concerns as she sent him on to kindergarten. He and his sister were separated and placed in different classes in kindergarten. Antoine felt lost from the beginning, both socially and academically. After the first marking period, he was considered to be below grade level in all areas.

His parents had multiple conferences with his teacher, who was doing her best to encourage Antoine. His parents hired a tutor and began giving extra support at home. The teacher felt other children excluded him because he did not want to participate. He started pulling out his hair, a disorder called trichotillomania, and became very withdrawn. His parents sought counseling, but Antoine was reluctant to report any problems. He said he liked school and his teacher.

Finally, the school decided to change classrooms and put him in his sister's classroom with a teacher with a different demeanor. Within a month, his performance improved, and by the end of the year, he was considered to be on grade level and obvious signs of stress—like the hair pulling—had disappeared. It wasn't clear whether the improvement came from being with his sister, a different group of children, or a new teacher, but Antoine's case shows the serious impact anxiety and stress can have on children.

ACTIVITY
STRENGTHS AND WEAKNESSES

Sit with your student and each make two lists—one of your strengths and one of areas that need improvement. Discuss your lists with each other and talk about any areas where you don't agree. From the list of areas that need improvement, each of you pick the easiest area to improve. Make a plan to improve the area using only strengths to improve it. Meet in several days to assess your progress and continue to monitor over time. When one area has been strengthened, choose another to strengthen.

Check out the example lists below:

Sarah's Strengths
- *I am creative and artistic.*
- *I love to read.*
- *I have a good group of friends.*

Sarah's Weaknesses
- *I hate going to math class.*
- *I get frustrated sometimes.*
- *I have trouble staying organized.*

Mom's Strengths
- *I am passionate about my job.*
- *I am dependable and organized.*
- *I am patient.*

Mom's Weaknesses
- *I am a perfectionist sometimes.*
- *I am not always at work on time.*

CHAPTER 7

Stress in the Community

You have brains in your head. You have feet in your shoes.
You can steer yourself any direction you choose.
You're on your own. And you know what you know.
And YOU are the one who'll decide where to go.
                    —Dr. Seuss, *Oh, the Places You'll Go*

KEY POINT: Stress is handled much better when children have a plan.

THINKING POINT: Am I limiting the media exposure my child has to stressful community events?

It's a big, big world. Sometimes that's exciting, sometimes it's challenging, and sometimes it's scary. Children not only need to learn how to process the things that happen in the world, but they also need to figure out their own place in it. That's hard work, some of the hardest work they'll ever do.

Table 3 demonstrates some of the ways children might demonstrate stress in response to things that happen around them.

Children experience two general kinds of community-related stress:

○ stress related to events going on around them over which they have very little control, and

○ stress related to everyday activities in their lives.

TABLE 3
EXAMPLES OF STRESS PRESENTATION

STRESS PRESENTATION IN YOUNGER CHILDREN (AGES 5–9)	STRESS PRESENTATION IN OLDER CHILDREN (AGES 10–12)
At a theme park, your child clings onto your leg and refuses to go near a large costumed character.	Your child has trouble falling asleep or is repeatedly woken by nightmares.
After learning about natural disasters (tornadoes, hurricanes, earthquakes), your child becomes terrified of thunderstorms.	After seeing a fire prevention film at school, your child begins to dwell on fears that her house will burn down.
During gymnastics, your child has a real urge and must go to the bathroom every 10 minutes.	On days there's a baseball game, your child develops a headache or stomachache.
After being toilet trained, your child reverts to childish behaviors like thumb sucking, being clingy, or bedwetting.	Your child bites his fingernails, pulls out his hair, or picks at his skin.

STRESS FROM WORLD EVENTS AND NATURAL DISASTERS

We live in a 24-hour news cycle. It's not the job of the news media to report the normal, safe lives most of us live every day. News crews report the unusual—the natural disasters, the acts of terrorism, the school shootings, the police shootings, and child abductions. It's frightening for all of us, but especially so for children, who lack the perspective that comes with age and maturity.

Most children believe that everything that exists in the world exists in *their* world. When a child sees news footage of a flood that washes away a village, the next logical assumption in his young mind is that a flood might come wash away *his* house. Small children, especially, can't put any distance between themselves and a scary event they see on television or hear adults discussing.

Dr. Phil McGraw, better known as Dr. Phil, offers two good rules (Dr. Phil, 2016) to parents about explaining the unexplainable to children. First, never ask kids to deal with adult issues. Second, don't ever allow them to feel responsible for things over which they have no influence and control (para. 1). Young kids often can't wrap their minds around terrorist attacks. If a terrorist attack occurs, you don't have to sit down and talk about it with your child; however, if your young child has an interest, give an age-appropriate explanation. You might say, "There are bad people in the world who are trying to hurt good people, but our president is doing everything possible to stop it from happening here."

When a frightening event occurs, here are some tools to help alleviate your child's stress.

First, try a hug. Wrapping your child up in your arms telegraphs the message that the world is safe and secure, and that you are there to protect and love her. A big bear hug provides physical contact and helps your child let go of tension, which makes it much easier for her to release emotional stress.

Maggie, a kindergarten teacher, tells about her student Max.

When Max came in to school one morning, something was off. When I told Max to put his backpack away, Max said "No!" and he threw himself on the floor and started to cry. After I got the other children situated, I went over to Max and asked, "What is wrong?" He said that he was worried about his mother, who was in the hospital, and he couldn't go to sleep the night before.

I told him I noticed something was wrong when he came to school today and was not smiling. He said, "Sorry." I told him, "You don't need to be sorry, and I hope your mom will be okay." Max said, "Yes, I was scared and worried." I told him, "I can understand because I stress out sometimes worrying about my mother or family." He looked at me and said, "Can I have a hug?" I agreed and gave him a great big hug, and Max's stress melted away.

Limit the child's exposure, especially to photographs, TV, and online media. This is a more-than-obvious step. Once your child gets a terrifying image in his head, it's hard to get it out. A child's imagination is capable of creating any number of scary scenarios. Jett's mom was shocked when her 5-year-old son said he was worried about being taken by a tsunami. It wasn't until later that she realized he was paying attention to the TV that was on while she prepared dinner. For the next few weeks, she frequently had to reassure Jett and explain that tsunamis don't happen in Florida and occur on the other side of the world. Sometimes an age-appropriate explanation is reassuring and is far less frightening than what is in his mind.

Put it all in perspective. Children will feel less stress about a far-away tragedy or disaster if they can understand the likelihood that it will not happen to them.

CONVERSATION STARTER
WHEN TRAGEDY STRIKES

When a local or national tragedy occurs, use these conversation starters, to help your child separate truth from fiction:

- ☐ Has this ever happened to us before?
- ☐ Do you know for certain this is going to happen? What proof do we have?
- ☐ Has this happened to anyone we know? If so, how did they handle it? Could we handle it the same way or differently?

Have a plan. One thing that helps manage stress is to take action. Here in South Florida, when a hurricane is threatening, there's a lot to do to get ready. Most stores provide a list of recommended supplies you should have on hand, and you can show this to your child. Together, you can bring in the patio furniture and the potted plants. You can show how you have gasoline for the backup generator and shutters for the windows to keep the whole family safe. Because the path of a hurricane's landfall is unpredictable, prepare your child ahead of time by explaining this may be just another stormy day or it could be a very strong storm with such high wind that the family may have to go into an inner room or to a shelter to keep everyone safe. Knowing what to expect helps children know they will be safe. If you know a particular issue is causing stress for your child, develop a written plan and walk through what to do if it ever happens. That can be very reassuring.

Find the good in the bad. With every tragedy comes an opportunity to help. If your child sees injured earthquake victims on the news, point out the rescue workers who appeared on the scene immediately. They'll see neighbors helping one another, or people traveling hundreds of miles to provide relief. Older children can also understand that if they are ever in need, people will come to their aid as well.

If age-appropriate, involve your child in providing aid. After the September 11 terrorist attacks, Jim's 8-year-old daughter and friends had a lemonade sale and donated the money to the local fire department. After the 2016 police shooting in Dallas, one family we know worked together to prepare and bring baked goods to the police department to express support. You can teach your child that every positive action nibbles away at very big problems.

STRESS FROM EVERYDAY LIFE

Every time your child goes out into the community, there's something new to manage. Your child will lead a much less stressful life if he feels confident of the following:

O He's not going to have to figure everything out all on his own.
O You'll help provide tools and answers as he grows and learns.
O It's okay not to know everything, and to make mistakes.

You might be surprised at some of the things our kids stress about. One 6-year-old, for instance, worried that when she grew up and got her driver's license, she wouldn't be able to find her way home or know the roads to take to get to her grandmother's house.

How might you reassure that little girl that she'd eventually be able to cope with the stress of driving alone? First, it's reassuring to remind a child that there's plenty of time to learn everything she needs to know. You might say:

Remember when you went to kindergarten, and you could only read a few words? But by the end of the year, you were reading whole books! Think of all you mastered in just one school year. You have more than 8 years to learn how to drive and how to get to Grandma's house and back home again.

Then, ask her to think of other tools that will help her. She might point out that your family car has a GPS, or that Grandma's house is just over a big hill, which is easy to remember. The idea is for her to think of all the tools that will be at her disposal, for this or anything else she finds stressful.

Let's look at some other real-world situations.

AT THE THEME PARK

Children have vivid imaginations. The younger they are, the more difficulty they have figuring out what's real and what's not. This explains why some children experience such stress in the presence of costumed characters. Your little boy may be crazy about the big, blue cookie-eating monster from the children's television show. Seeing that same character in person, about 6 feet tall, can easily cause a child's heart to pound and send his stress level through the roof. Why? Because seeing Cookie Monster on a TV screen is normal. Seeing a ginormous Cookie Monster in person isn't, and can be very upsetting to a child.

Similarly, young children still can't process the idea of imaginary danger. All danger is real to them. So when they see a storybook villain in person at a theme park, all of their senses go on high alert. They might refuse to go anywhere near the character, not just to protect themselves, but to protect you, too.

AT THE MOVIES

Unexpected things can frighten children, and seeing them on the big screen can be overwhelming. Let's say that a year ago, your child got separated from you on a crowded street, even for just a minute. It was terrifying for both of you. Watching a movie scene set on a busy sidewalk can make your child experience the event all over again, right down to feeling physical panic or wanting to scream or cry. Always be willing to leave the theater if your child seems to be experiencing this kind of response.

Be alert if your child covers his eyes or buries his face in your shoulder during a film. Movies, especially in theaters, provide an enormous amount of visual stimulation, and every child has a different physical and emotional tolerance level. Some children will find scary movies funny, some will enjoy being scared, and still others will cry. Don't presume that an animated movie is safe for a sensitive child; animated violence can provoke strong emotional and physical responses in a child.

DOCTOR AND DENTAL VISITS

When you anticipate something scary, your body can react the very same way as if you're actually experiencing it. This is one of the reasons some children respond so intensely and negatively to the idea of visiting the doctor or the dentist. When they imagine it, they're already experiencing the physical fear or anxiety. They don't like it and they want it to stop.

One approach that's sometimes helpful is to point out how visiting the doctor and dentist helps all of us stay healthy. Many children secretly worry that there's something wrong with them, that they'll get sick or even die. They worry about getting a shot and about how much it can hurt. Your child might actively resist going to a health practitioner specifically because she doesn't want to get bad news. So, if your child shows stress at the idea of a visit to the pediatrician, don't presume it's only because she is afraid of the pain of getting a shot. Ask open-ended questions and learn specifically what is behind the fear.

Also, give your child some measure of control. Make sure you find a healthcare practitioner your child likes and trusts, who listens and offers genuine reassurance.

STRANGERS

A lot of us grew up with the admonition, "Never talk to strangers." But our parents didn't really mean that, did they? If we never talked to strangers, we'd never have made friends; we'd be rude and antisocial.

Some children are social butterflies who thrive in new environments. Some cling tightly to Mom's leg and shake at the thought of meeting someone new. Still others are fearful of the strangers because they secretly fear being abducted. If your child shows signs of stress at meeting new people, make sure you understand what, precisely, distresses them.

As parents, we must help our children stay safe, but understand that not all strangers pose a threat. We can teach even the shyest child the art of meeting a new person. They can make eye contact, because you can learn a lot about a person by looking them in the eye. Then, they can ask themselves, "Do I trust this person?" If not, their stress response may be giving them valuable information.

SPORTS AND SOCIAL ACTIVITIES

Our kids are under more stress than ever to do more and be better. What happens when your son tells you he feels sick to his stomach before every basketball game, or your daughter has to use the bathroom five times before leaving for a birthday party? Physical symptoms like nausea, vomiting, headache, stomachache, sleeplessness, or the frequent need to urinate can all be signs of stress in a child. If you notice a connection between symptoms like these and a particular sport or activity, it might be a stress response.

If you think this is the case in your home, make sure you are your child's biggest fan, not her biggest critic. Many children feel extreme stress if they perceive that they've disappointed their parents. Practice together so your child has a chance to develop his skills. This could mean throwing a football in the yard or staging a party at home to work on social skills. The more children develop their abilities, the more confidence (and less stress) they are likely to feel.

BE THE BEST EXAMPLE YOU CAN BE

A little stress can lead to achievement. A lot of stress can lead to brokenness. Your child will take his cue from you and how you react to the world. Here are a few closing suggestions on helping your child learn to navigate the real stresses we face every day.

Live a healthy life. Stress begs to be relieved. It needs an outlet or it becomes damaging to our bodies and our minds. If you respond to a tough day by pouring an enormous glass of wine, eating half a chocolate layer cake, or kicking the dog, your child will see that as an acceptable way to relieve stress. Instead, if you run on the treadmill or talk through the day's events with your spouse, you're modeling a different and healthier approach.

Show your child how to manage a stressful situation in a positive way. When you hit unexpected traffic and you're running late, how you respond to the situation will teach your child a lot. It will either teach your child to freak out, drive aggressively, pound the steering wheel in frustration, curse, or take it in stride with grace and patience. You might point out what you might have done to help alleviate the stress of the situation by saying something like, "You know, if we'd left a few minutes earlier, I wouldn't be so stressed about getting stuck in traffic. Note to self: I need to remember to do that next time."

Teach the difference between a real crisis and something that just feels that way. When was the last time you had a day when absolutely nothing stressful happened? Me neither. But it's very rare that we face real, true emergencies. Children fret easily about things; their hearts race, it gets hard for them to think, and they may want to cry. In their bodies, it feels just like a real emergency. Help them take minor setbacks in stride by showing them how you adapt to the small stresses in your own life.

RESOURCES

GOING TO THE DENTIST

The Berenstain Bears Visit the Dentist by Stan Berenstain and Jan Berenstain (ages 3–7) is a classic book for helping calm kids' fears of going to the dentist.

Just Going to the Dentist by Mercer Mayer (ages 3–7) helps kids learn going to the dentist is not so bad.

Going to the Dentist by Anne Civardi (ages 3+) helps explain the first trip to a dentist.

Curious George Visits the Dentist by H. A. Rey (ages 4–7) helps children learn about dental hygiene and going to the dentist.

GOING TO THE DOCTOR

The Berenstain Bears Go to the Doctor by Stan Berenstain and Jan Berenstain (ages 3–7) is a classic book to teach children what happens when they go to the doctor.

Franklin Goes to the Hospital by Paulette Bourgeois (ages 3–8) helps children know when they are scared they can still feel brave.

Say Ahhh!: Dora Goes to the Doctor by Phoebe Beinstein (ages 3–7) helps children understand going to the doctor.

Lions Aren't Scared of Shots by Howard J. Bennett (ages 8–12) helps children deal with the fear of getting a shot.

FEAR OF SLEEPING ALONE

Mommy, I Want to Sleep in Your Bed! by Harriet Ziefert (ages 3–7) explains how Charlie learns to sleep alone.

I Love to Sleep in My Own Bed by Shelley Admont (ages 2–7) is Jimmy the bunny's adventure for learning to sleep alone.

Night Light: A Story for Children Afraid of the Dark by Jack Dutro (ages 4–9) depicts how Kalispel learns to face his fear of daylight.

Scary Night Visitors: A Story for Children With Bedtime Fears by Irene Wineman Marcus and Paul Marcus (ages 4–8) helps parents and children handle bedtime fears.

I Sleep in My Own Bed by Glenn Wright (ages 4+) deals with the fear of sleeping in bed alone or having a bad dream.

MONSTER FEAR

The Berenstain Bears and the Bad Dream by Stan Berenstain and Jan Berenstain (ages 3–7) teaches children that dreams can be scary but are not real.

The Berenstain Bears in the Dark by Stan Berenstain and Jan Berenstain (fear of the dark; ages 3–7) is a classic book for teaching children how to overcome fears.

There's a Nightmare in My Closet by Mercer Mayer (ages 3–5) is a classic for helping children understand nightmares.

Franklin in the Dark by Paulette Bourgeois (fear of the dark; ages 3–8) helps children learn how to come out of their shell.

CHAPTER 8

Stress in the Family

Wish we could turn back time, to the good old days
When our momma sang us to sleep but now we're stressed
out.

—Twenty One Pilots, "Stressed Out"

KEY POINT: Stress in the family is manageable when you've shown your child ways of coping with the stress.

THINKING POINT: Do I have boundaries in place that provide loving limits that help my child to understand the parameters that he or she can operate within?

Stress takes a heavy toll on our kids. At home, your child's stress-related behavior is not your child being spoiled. It's not merely your child having a bad attitude. Stress is your child's body reacting to stressors in life. It's important to remember that distress does not spontaneously go away. If significant stressors are occurring in your family, your child may show some of the signs detailed in Table 4.

The support you provide your child matters. According to researchers Masten and Coastworth (1998), who studied stress and resiliency in children, "Children who do well have adults who care for them, brains that are developing normally, and, as they grow older, the ability to manage their own attention, emotions, and

TABLE 4

SIGNS OF STRESS AT HOME

STRESS PRESENTATION IN YOUNGER CHILDREN (AGES 5–9)	STRESS PRESENTATION IN OLDER CHILDREN (AGES 10–12)
Your child shows very high energy and silly behavior as if to say, "Hey everyone, cheer up!"	He or she may become angry at the ones causing the stress.
Your child may become nervous and pace around, clench hands, or pick at nails.	Your child may be acting out verbally or physically.
Your little one may retreat to a quiet space or try to be alone.	Stress may affect your child's ability to eat, and he or she will have a variable appetite.
Sometimes young children become very quiet and refuse to talk.	Your child may become withdrawn.

behavior" (p. 215). You are an important influence in helping your child know how to bounce back from a stressful situation.

YOUR FAMILY

Each family is unique. There are certain routines, rituals, or traditions that make your family who they are. Can you think of one? In Jim's family, they had a bedtime ritual of saying bedtime prayers and then stating, "I love you to the moon and back." Then, the child would say, "I love you to the stars and back," and there would be several rounds of seeing who could out-love the other. This was a fun way to end the day on a positive note.

No family is perfect, including each of ours. Stress enters the family through everyday life events. You stress about money, work, health, or your relationship with your spouse or significant other. When your child or children enter the world, they bring joy, but, at times, stress. If you've traveled with your child, you understand. If you've battled with your child over completing homework, you understand. If you have pleaded, argued, and threatened your child about going to school, you understand. Stress affects the whole family.

When one person is stressed, it often has a ripple effect, and the stress spreads to other family members. John, a sweet 6 year old, put it this way, "I just want my happy mom back and not my angry mom." John felt his mom's stress, and it created worry. Children react in different ways to stress. John became withdrawn and nervous whereas other children his age may become angry. Your child's behavior has a purpose, so by tuning into your child's behavior you can often decipher the message your child is sending.

High energy is one way children react to stress. When Jen's 4-year-old son sensed stress, he became very active and ran around, sticking his butt out at family members and stating, "I'm farting on you." Most of the time, his silly behavior helped diffuse the stress and bring a smile to family members' faces, but he didn't know when to stop, so eventually Jen had to tell him.

FAMILY EXPECTATIONS

What do you expect of your child? Very few of us get a free ride, so having expectations teaches your child how to be a contributing member of a family unit. Most parents expect their children to be respectful to everyone including siblings, help in the household chores, and take responsibility in their schoolwork. These expectations set the stage for a child's behavior and provide boundaries that help children feel safe.

CONVERSATION STARTER
HOUSE RULES

Most families have unspoken house rules, but written rules can help children clearly understand expectations. If you've never created written family rules, try it. Ask your child, "What are our house rules? What's the most important rule in our home? How should someone respond if they notice a rule isn't being followed?"

These rules apply to adults as well as children. Jim's family rules were: *Say nice things to each other with no name-calling. Help each other. Do what was asked the first time. Pick up your stuff.*

SET REALISTIC EXPECTATIONS

Sometimes parents expect more than a child is capable of producing. An unrealistic expectation of your child creates stress. Unrealistic expectations may take the form of straight A's, prefect penmanship, being a star athlete, keeping clothes perfectly clean, or behaving like a little adult. Sorry to tell you, but you may be one cause of your child's stress. Below summarizes a conversation from one married husband and wife about their 12-year-old son's grades.

Dad: He's just lazy and not trying hard enough.

Mom: He does work hard, but you aren't always home to see it. We should be okay with C's because his effort is there, but sometimes I wonder if he just isn't smart. We may need to have him tested.

Dad: Let's not do that yet. It's his motivation. I'll tell him that if he gets all A's and B's, then he can get that new video game system he has been asking for.

Mom: What if he doesn't do it? You and I weren't always A, B students, so let's not expect that from him.

Dad: That's true, but I just want him to have plenty of opportunities in the future.

Mom: I agree.

This conversation highlights the concern of many parents; you want your child to have opportunities to get into a good school, college, or career. If you know your child is working hard but is still not performing to your expectations, begin by having an honest conversation with your child. Most children don't excel at all academic subjects. Focus on the effort, and if your child's effort was at 100%, a C grade is acceptable. Ask questions such as, "Are you satisfied with your grades? What can we do to help you? What makes this subject challenging for you?"

DON'T COMPARE

If you have more than one child, you've compared the two; it's natural. Yet, your children are different beings, so one child may have higher capabilities and one lower. We encourage you to do your best not to compare them. At least don't compare them out loud or in front of one another. Children stress when parents push them to become something they don't have the talent or passion for doing. Certainly you should expose your child to different activities and, if she joins a team, have her stick it out until the end of the season because this teaches a valuable lesson on taking responsibility. But recognize her passions.

Help explore passions through volunteer experiences, online videos, and books. If you don't have preconceived ideas of what your child should become, you won't be disappointed. As his son grew, Mike always expected his Cole to go to college, but as his son aged, his passion was playing guitar. Mike and his wife nurtured this through lessons. When Cole was a senior, Mike and his wife realized college was their dream but not Cole's dream and agreed to his one-year band tour upon graduation. Mike jokes that when Cole was 6, if you had told him that his son would become a traveling musician after high school, he would have said, "You're crazy." Most successful individuals are passionate about what they do, so continue to identify your child's passion.

OVERSCHEDULING

Many children today are overscheduled, and this creates stress for them and you. Consider 7-year-old Ethan. He attends school, goes to aftercare, is picked up just before 6 p.m., eats a drive-thru dinner, has an hour of sports practice, arrives home, showers, works on homework, and collapses into bed, exhausted from his day. The next day, he does it all again, but instead of sports practice he may go to music lessons, Hebrew school, or tutoring. On the weekend, there are games, recitals, more practices, and when there is finally downtime, his parents wonder why Ethan can't entertain himself. His parents have missed the value of play and creative time.

WHEN YOUR CHILD HAS A DISABILITY

Having a child with a disability presents unique financial, friendship, learning, and emotional struggles that create stress for your child and you. Children with a disability such as autism, ADHD, dyslexia, or a learning disability often stress and believe they are dumb. If your child has expressed this sentiment to you, use books to help give your child understanding that he is not stupid or alone in his struggles. Based on his personal and professional experiences, Jim wrote children's books to explain learning disabilities and ADHD. You can read these books to your child to provide understanding and hope for the future:

- O *Terrific Teddy and the b-d Mix-Up* (dyslexia)
- O *Terrific Teddy's Excessive Energy* (ADHD)
- O *Terrific Teddy's Writing Wars* (dysgraphia)

CONVERSATION STARTER
EXPLAINING LEARNING DIFFERENCES

Tell your child: "Sit with me while I read you this really good book." Read whichever book about Teddy that is appropriate for your child's disability.

Afterward, ask: "What did you think about Teddy? How did he feel? Yes, he felt worried, but after his parents got him the right help he felt a lot better. Was there anything about Teddy that was like you? You're my Terrific Teddy, and I love you so much!"

DIVORCE

When parents divorce, children are confused and will have a lot of worries and concerns about the divorce. They stress about what is going to happen to them. Continue to give your child the reassuring message that you are there to listen and help. If your child is stressed, ask her to apply these four steps:

- O Recognize how you are feeling.
- O Ask yourself, "Where is this feeling coming from?"

○ Apply a strategy (e.g., draw, journal, playdough pound) to appropriately express how you feel.
○ Let the feeling go so you can move on.

Ideally, you'd maintain a coparenting relationship with your ex-spouse so you both can help your child apply these steps, always keeping in mind the best interest of the child.

Children of divorce fare better with an active coping style. This implies you should not ignore the divorce or how the family changed. You'll increase your child's ability to cope and adjust to divorce more quickly by helping your child apply problem solving and positive restructuring of the new situation. An excerpt Maria gave her son was, "Even though Dad's not living with us, he still loves you, and now Mommy and Daddy are not fighting, and we don't have to worry about Daddy's moods." She told us her child appeared somewhat relieved that the home situation would not be as stressful.

STRATEGIES TO HELP YOUR CHILD COPE WITH THE STRESS OF DIVORCE

Draw pictures. Your child's feelings can be expressed through art. This process helps children express themselves in a positive manner and allows you to know what your child is feeling concerning the divorce. Look at your child's picture and ask questions including:
○ How does divorce make you feel?
○ What color shows how you feel?
○ Which part of the picture is most important to you?

Do playdough pounding. Playdough pounding helps children release emotions. Purchase or make playdough. Allow your child to roll, build, or squish it. Then, tell your child to pound the playdough with his fist and complete these sentences:
○ I'm angry about the divorce because . . .
○ When I think about my family I feel . . .
○ I'm scared about the divorce because . . .
○ I'm worried about . . .

Blow bubbles. Most children enjoy blowing bubbles, so try this with a stress-busting twist. When your child is feeling stressed, pull out the bottle of bubbles and teach her to blow bubbles with slow, gentle, and controlled breathing. She should take a deep breath and slowly let it out as she blows a stream of bubbles. This helps with relaxation.

RESOURCES

Two Homes by Claire Masurel (ages 3–7) follows Alex's journey of setting up special features at each parent's home.

It's Not Your Fault, Koko Bear by Vicki Lansky (ages 3–7) is a story about a loveable bear who doesn't want two homes but learns how to make the best of it.

My Family's Changing by Pat Thomas (ages 4–7) also includes questions to help children process what they are going through.

I Am Living in 2 Homes by Garcelle Beauvais (ages 4–7) follows twins as they learn the benefits of having two homes.

When Mom and Dad Divorce by Emily Menendez-Aponte (ages 8–12) helps children deal with the emotions they experience during divorce.

A NEW BABY

The addition of a sibling can be an exciting time for young children but simultaneously stressful. Following the birth of a younger sibling, your older child may begin to fear he is less important when, of course, this is not true. Yet, keep in mind it's what your child perceives that matters. Prepare your child for the new sibling through discussions about what changes may occur in the family. During the baby shower, ask a relative to bring a gift for your older child. Upon birth, make it a special day for your older child by having a "big brother" or "big sister" party.

STRATEGIES TO HELP YOUR CHILD COPE WITH THE STRESS OF A NEW SIBLING

Use deep breathing exercises. Teach your child how to slowly take a deep breath while silently counting to five and then slowly release it as she counts from 6 to 10.

Listen to relaxing music. This especially helps young children.

Go to a quiet space. Teach your child to go to a quiet space where the baby is not allowed and where the child has special things she does not have to share with the baby.

Sing a song. Your child can sing "You Are My Sunshine" or a similar song or recite common nursery rhymes either aloud or silently.

Have special gifts. Purchase "big brother" or "big sister" gifts to give your child as friends and relatives start showing up with baby gifts, so your older child won't feel left out.

Point out the benefits. Being an older child has benefits, like choosing what to eat, being able to go the park and play, and having friends.

RESOURCES

Big Brother Now: A Story About Me and Our New Baby by Annette Sheldon (ages 2–5) demonstrates how children can still feel loved moving from being an only child to a big brother.

Big Sister Now: A Story About Me and Our New Baby by Annette Sheldon (ages 2–5) features Kate's feelings about welcoming a baby brother.

The Berenstain Bears' New Baby by Stan Berenstain and Jan Berenstain (ages 3–7) helps children adjust to new life with a baby.

The Berenstain Bears and Baby Makes Five by Stan Berenstain and Jan Berenstain (ages 3–7) depicts adjustments siblings make when Honey, the baby, comes and wants all of the attention.

The New Baby by Mercer Mayer (ages 3–7) follows Little Critter's adjustment to a new sibling.

Elana's Ears, or How I Became the Best Big Sister in the World by Gloria Roth Lowell (ages 3–8) features a girl adjusting to being a big sister who learns her baby sister can't hear.

MOVING

Moving to a new home creates stress—even if the new home is within the same town. The perceived fear of the unknown can create stress. Your child's room will feel different even though furniture and belongings may have remained the same. When moving, added stressors for children include leaving old friends behind and making new friends, along with changing schools. As much as possible, prepare your child to deal with the stressors of moving.

STRATEGIES TO HELP YOUR CHILD COPE WITH THE STRESS OF MOVING

Share your experience. Most of us had to move when we were children so tell your child about your experience. When you share your experiences with your child, it creates warmth and intimacy that comfort your child because he understands you are grounded in having been through the same process as a child.

Document. Take pictures of friends and familiar places and offer ways to keep in contact with close friends via phone, e-mail, and letters. Help your child talk about what he or she will miss and about what will be new and different.

Keep away on move-in day. During the actual move-out and move-in process, kids feel like they are in the way. Take steps to hire a babysitter, or ask a close friend or relative to help watch your child at their home. Your stress during the move will be lower and so will your child's stress.

Unpack your child first. Set up your child's new room first. This helps your child get settled in right away with familiar belongings.

RESOURCES

Big Ernie's New Home: A Story for Young Children Who Are Moving by Teresa Martin and Whitney Martin (ages 2–5) follows children's feelings of anxiety and sadness during a move.

Boomer's Big Day by Constance W. McGeorge (ages 3–6) helps children explore their feelings of confusion and concern on moving day.

My Very Exciting, Sorta Scary, Big Move: A Workbook for Children Moving to a New Home by Lori Attanasio Woodring (ages 5–11) is a workbook that walks children through the steps of moving.

DEATH OF FAMILY MEMBER OR RELATIVE

When a family member dies, it creates stress for the entire family unit. You are stressed, and your child is, too. Your child may also feel uncertainty, fear, and may even believe he somehow contributed to the person's death. These can be difficult and uncomfortable conversations, but give your child an honest, concise, and age-appropriate explanation. Don't be afraid to give your child an explanation using the words *dead* or *died*. During the initial explaining, avoid saying confusing statements to children such as, "Grandpa has gone home." Young children will want you to give the same explanation many times because it offers reassurance. This is how one dad explained it:

> I have something very serious to tell you. Mom died today. This means her body stopped working and she can't feel, hear, breathe, talk, or hug us anymore. Most people live a long life, and I plan on being here to take care of you. You're going to have a lot of questions, and I'm here to answer them and we'll be doing some other things to help you, too.

STRATEGIES TO HELP YOUR CHILD COPE WITH THE STRESS OF A FAMILY MEMBER'S DEATH

Draw a family picture. Have your child complete statements such as:
- *Some things I enjoyed doing with my ____ were ____.*
- *My ____ liked these things: ____.*
- *Some questions I have are ____.*
- *What I miss most about my ____ is ____.*

Reassure your child it's good to keep talking about the person who died and it's how you keep memories alive. Talking to your child about the loved one will not scar the child or make him feel too sad. You want to encourage communication, and if your child is not comfortable talking, then encourage him to draw.

Recognize feelings. Help your child recognize the feelings he is experiencing in his body. Use paper to draw an outline of your child's body. Next, discuss the physical ways your child feels, and use a different color to represent each feeling. For example, your child may feel nervous butterflies in the stomach, sweaty palms, a sensation of being spaced out, a broken heart, or tired eyes.

RESOURCES

Sad Isn't Bad: A Good-Grief Guidebook for Kids Dealing With Loss by Michaelene Mundy (ages 4–8) contains positive affirmations to help children deal with loss.

I Miss You: A First Look at Death by Pat Thomas (ages 4–8) helps children deal with feelings experienced when someone close to them dies.

I'll Always Love You by Hans Wilhelm (ages 3–7) follows a boy when his dog, Elfie, dies.

TERMINAL ILLNESS

When a family member is diagnosed with a terminal illness, life becomes a whirlwind of doctor's appointments, treatments, quiet time for resting, phone calls, and family visits. During this time, stress takes a toll on your entire family unit. Your child will be hurting, so it's important not to overlook signs of stress because much of the focus will be on the ill parent. Even if your child appears to be handling things just fine, the stress may be just beneath the surface and waiting to erupt.

STRATEGIES TO HELP YOUR CHILD COPE WITH THE STRESS OF TERMINAL ILLNESS

Ask leading questions. Children often think in literal terms, so when your child asks a question, you can gain valuable insight into his or her thought process if you ask something to the effect of, "That's a good question, and I'm wondering: What got you thinking about that?"

Draw upon your faith. If you are a family of faith, lean into and draw strength if you believe that death is temporal, not eternal, and that we will be reunited with each other again.

Plan. Give your child an age-appropriate explanation of how life and death work. Explain how her loved one's body will stop working. Children who understand what will happen after their parent's death will be spared some of the worry about the unknown.

RESOURCES

Help Me Say Goodbye: Activities for Helping Kids Cope When a Special Person Dies by Janis Silverman (ages 3+) is for kids whose family member is sick or dies.

Where Did Mommy's Superpowers Go? by Jenifer Gershman (ages 3+) helps children understand cancer.

TAKE CONTROL OF STRESS IN THE FAMILY

Stress is all around, but how you frame or approach it makes a difference. Your child will feel empowered when you teach him or her strategies for dealing with stress. Interventions give children control and a sense of "I can deal with this."

STRATEGIES TO HELP YOUR CHILD TAKE CONTROL OF STRESS

Create a menu. Create a coping menu using the strategies listed below. You can discuss the strategies and then write the top three on an index card that could be placed in your child's binder, backpack, or pocket. Your child can pick which technique works best:

- Drawing pictures
- Pounding playdough
- Blowing bubbles
- Using deep breathing
- Listening to relaxing music
- Going to a quiet space

○ Singing a song
○ Using a stress thermometer
○ Using statements like "I'm the boss of my fear"

Create a stress thermometer. A stress thermometer (see Figure 1) helps a child identify how stressed he or she feels from low to high. A simple 3-point scale suffices for helping most children recognize when he or she feels low, medium, or high stress. Practice using the stress thermometer using these role-plays:

> **Parent:** I want you to imagine you are in some stressful situations. As I read them to you, tell me where each would go on the thermometer: low, medium, or high stress. You are in school and your teacher tells the class to get your lunch box and line up for class, but you realize you left your lunch box at home! Is this low, medium, or high stress? What would you do?
>
> **Child:** Responses will vary, but this is usually medium to high stress. The child could ask the teacher to borrow money or give the cafeteria an IOU to get lunch today and pay tomorrow.
>
> **Parent:** Here's the next one: Imagine you get to sports practice and your coach asks each child for the signed permission form, but you don't have yours because it was in your dad's car and he's not here. Is this low, medium, or high stress? What would you do?
>
> **Child:** Responses will vary, but this is usually low stress. The child could ask the coach if the form could be turned in at the next practice or if the coach could text the parent to work it out.

Create a "worry page." When a stressful situation occurs, you or your child can write it down. Later, when your child is relaxed, discuss the worry. Work with your child to teach her how to identify what caused the worry. Were there certain thoughts in her mind that perpetuated her worry? What could she have told herself to cancel out the worry?

Teach "I'm the Boss." Your child can learn he can boss his fear away. Teach your child to say, "I am stronger than the_____. That

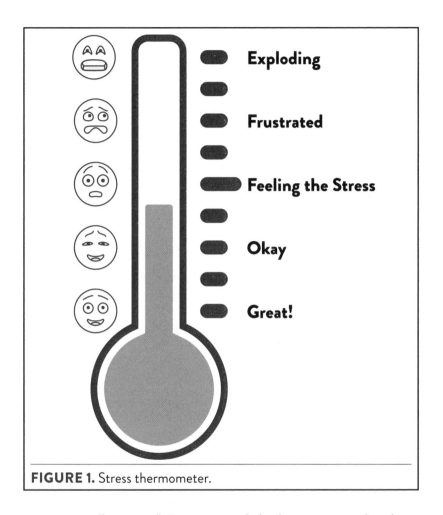

FIGURE 1. Stress thermometer.

_____ will go away." Some parents help draw a picture that shows their child being stronger than the fear.

Create a chant. Teach your child how to reassure herself by practicing this phrase: "My name is _____ and I am okay." When your child is faced with a stressor she can immediately begin this positive chant and continue to repeat it until the stress has subsided. This chant empowers your child.

Create a written emergency plan. Preparing your child with knowledge of what to do in a stressful situation helps alleviate stress of the unknown. Many families teach their child what to do if there were a fire in the home. Children must know how to safely get away from the fire and know where to meet up with the rest of the family. Other families discuss and plan for what to do if there were a national emergency while your child is in school. Use available free resources such as those found at https://www.ready.gov/kids/parents to create a written emergency plan for your family.

Color. Coloring is therapeutic and relaxing and is enjoyed by children and adults alike (Curry & Kasser, 2005). Use coloring books to help your child change her focus from a sense of worry to calm. This is also a wonderful activity to share with your child. Coloring together can provide a wonderful opportunity for conversation, in addition to serving as a healthy coping mechanism for handling the stress of the day.

Stress Busters

CHAPTER 9

Protection From Stress

You're braver than you believe, and stronger than you seem, and smarter than you think.
—Christopher Robin, *Pooh's Grand Adventure: The Search for Christopher Robin*

> **KEY POINT:** How children view themselves and assess situations has a huge impact on the outcomes.
>
> **THINKING POINT:** Does my child have a *fixed* or a *growth* mindset? If it is a *fixed* mindset, how can I encourage him to understand that effort can result in change and growth?

Given our current environment with stressors practically everywhere you turn, helping your children develop protective factors that boost their immunity to succumbing to negative impacts of stress is one of the most important things you can do for them. In many cases, how a child thinks about himself and how he views a situation have a huge impact on the outcome.

Protective factors considered to help deflect or manage stress include:

- development of personal characteristics like resiliency and flexibility,
- a tendency toward optimism,
- a sense of humor,

○ having a growth mindset, and
○ a nurturing environment at home and school that is supportive, has structure, and provides opportunities for growth and success.

RESILIENCY AND FLEXIBILITY

To put it simply—think about resiliency as a person's ability to be knocked down, get back up, and keep on fighting. A resilient person is a problem solver who usually takes things in stride. At the highest level, a resilient person views difficulties as challenges or learning opportunities that can be instructive. Dr. Robert Brooks (2015) has written extensively on resilience and emphasized "the concept of 'personal control' as a key dimension of resilience. To be resilient, we must examine the steps we can initiate to deal successfully with the struggles and challenges we face" (para. 15). In *Raising Resilient Children*, Brooks and Goldstein (2001) wrote that resilient children "have developed the ability to solve problems and make decisions and thus are more likely to view mistakes, hardships, and obstacles as challenges to confront rather than stressors to avoid" (p. 5).

Obviously most children won't automatically view disappointments and mistakes that way—it will take years of maturity and insight, as well as assistance and good examples set by the adults around them. Resiliency has a lot to do with temperament and self-control, so some children will require much more support in their development of resiliency than others. If your child is rigid, perfectionistic, has low self-esteem, or suffers from ADHD and its accompanying executive functioning problem, adjusting to disappointments may be a journey requiring patience and perseverance on your part! Children on the autism spectrum particularly have difficulty developing resiliency.

If *rigid* is a word you could use to describe your child, remember that is the way he or she copes with the world and manages his or her environment. Structure and predictability are ways to maintain some control over the environment. It goes much deeper than defiant behavior. Oftentimes the child lacks coping skills to deal with change and benefits from supports. These supports can include help in planning an alternate activity if plans fall through, talking them through what the change will entail, giving them time to prepare for the change, or reminding them of strategies that help them cope with difficult situations like breathing, visualizing themselves in a calm place, listening to music, going to a quiet place, or participating in some kind of physical activity.

As a parent, it is often easier to expend significant energy on ensuring things go the way your child planned than cope with the fallout a disruption in plans brings. However, it is important to gradually introduce change into his rigid world while teaching skills to handle the changes.

As an example, Marty had to cancel her son's visit to the zoo because she had to take her car in for service instead. Her son, Jacob, was obsessed with animals and had been looking forward to the trip for weeks. As soon as Marty found out about her car problems, she sat Jacob down, got out the calendar, and explained they would have to pick an alternate day for the zoo trip. He cried, but Marty helped him understand what had happened to the car. They rescheduled the trip, and Jacob entered it on his mom's calendar. To reward him for not having a full-fledged temper tantrum, Marty helped Jacob plan an additional zoo activity that they had not originally planned to do, feeding the otters. The actual car repair took less time than expected, so Jacob also got to go to the library to select some books about animals. Marty helped him see that some positive things came out of their change of plans.

Psychologist Dr. Michael J. Poulin's research (Poulin, Brown, Dillard, & Smith, 2013) suggested that helping others has a positive impact on stress reduction (p. 1). Using his research, Stanford University psychologist Dr. Kelly McGonigal (2013) concluded, "Caring created resilience." A practical implication of this research suggests that involving your children in projects that help others can assist them in becoming resilient themselves. Brainstorm with them some needs they have observed in the community that they might be able to help with or help them think of ongoing projects they could do. Donating unused toys or clothing to shelters or food to a food bank could be easy ways to involve them in helping others, as well as give them some perspective about others' needs.

In her TED talk, McGonigal (2013) also said that the oxytocin secreted by the pituitary gland during stress can actually cause people to be more social—either seeking or giving support. She concluded by saying that by changing your mind about stress, you could change the way it impacts you.

The timing of conversations with your child about resiliency will be critical. Oftentimes after a big disappointment, children are so emotional that they cannot think rationally about an alternate plan or how to deal with the disappointment. If that is the case, let your child know you want to talk about it at a later time. Either let him initiate it or bring it up again yourself in a calm, relaxed environment. You might begin by sharing an experience from your own life about a setback and how you did not let that define you. As we have said before, you can be your child's most effective model.

CONVERSATION STARTER
WHEN PLANS CHANGE

Tell your child: "I know you were really counting on _____. I am just as sorry as you are that it did not happen as you expected. I wonder what you were feeling at that point. How do you feel about it now?"

If your child can't label his feelings, work with him to develop that vocabulary. Feeling words that might be descriptive are angry, frustrated, sad, powerless, or defeated. If he can't identify his feelings, work with him to recognize and identify each one.

Then, and most importantly, ask, "What can you do to get over those feelings and make the situation better?" For example, if a friend cancelled out on a much anticipated play date, explore his feelings. Did he feel sad, hurt, or afraid that his friend did not want to play with him anymore?

Depending on the answer, make another plan—either invite the friend again, arrange another play date, or think of an alternate activity that will be fun.

RESOURCES

Is a Worry Worrying You? by Ferida Wolff (ages 4–8) stresses understanding worries and using creative problem solving.

What Do You Do With a Problem? by Kobi Yamada (ages 4–8) encourages seeing the possibilities in problems.

The Girl Who Never Made Mistakes by Mark Pett and Gary Rubinstein (ages 4–8) features a 9-year-old girl who makes her first mistake in a very public way.

The Hugging Tree: A Story About Resilience by Jill Neimark (ages 5–8) teaches children about hope and resilience.

Bounce Back: How to Be a Resilient Kid by Wendy L. Moss (ages 8–12) builds resiliency skills.

OPTIMISM

In our practices, some children often go to the negative while others are always positive—the old glass half full or half empty concept. If your child is a Negative Nelly, it will take lots of hard work to get her to reframe her thinking. Cognitive behavior therapy is offered by therapists to help children reframe their thoughts. Caveat: If a child is depressed, he may be unable to see the positive in situations without treatment and cognitive behavior therapy.

One way to help your child focus on the positive is to use family mealtime for all family members to discuss the "best part of their day." Of course, if upsetting things have happened, you will want to discuss them as well. However, focusing on the positive hopefully helps your child be on the lookout for something to discuss at dinner.

RESOURCES

How Full Is Your Bucket? For Kids by Tom Rath and Mary Rekmeyer (ages 3–8) introduces the concept of creating happiness by doing nice things for others.

Be Positive!: A Book About Optimism by Cheri J. Meiners (ages 4–8) helps children discover how choices they make can lead to happiness and feeling capable.

Did I Ever Tell You How Lucky You Are? by Dr. Seuss (ages 5–9) features Dr. Seuss's optimism.

What to Do When You Grumble Too Much: A Kid's Guide to Overcoming Negativity by Dawn Huebner (ages 6–12) shows children different ways to respond to life's ups and downs.

How to Get Unstuck From the Negative Muck: A Kid's Guide to Getting Rid of Negative Thinking by Lake Sullivan presents cognitive behavioral therapy strategies and includes journal exercises for kids.

SENSE OF HUMOR

The ability to laugh at ourselves does a number of things. It releases endorphins, it momentarily removes the seriousness of a situation, which might allow for some perspective, and it enables us to engage with others. Some of us are naturally more humorous than others. If you and your family are not known for a sense of humor, try keeping a humor notebook or computer file. Include jokes, cartoons, and humorous incidents. Model for your child how effective it can be to laugh at your mistakes rather than crumbling under the embarrassment of them.

RESOURCES

Kids Who Laugh: How to Develop Your Child's Sense of Humor by Louis R. Franzini examines the humor and gives parents suggestions to help their child with laughter.

The Day the Crayons Quit by Drew Daywalt (ages 3–7) features Duncan, a young boy who gets creative letters from his crayons.

Scholastic Reader Level 1: Get the Giggles: A First Joke Book by Bronwen Davies (ages 4–7) has multiple jokes to be enjoyed by all.

The Book With No Pictures by B. J. Novak (ages 5–8) is a funny book with silly made-up words that the person reading the book has to read aloud.

Laugh-Out-Loud Jokes for Kids by Rob Elliott (ages 7–10) features jokes children enjoy.

Just Joking: 300 Hilarious Jokes, Tricky Tongue Twisters, and Ridiculous Riddles by National Geographic Kids (ages 7–10) features tongue twisters, riddles, and jokes.

ACTIVITY

CREATING REMINDERS ON HOW TO HANDLE STRESS

Sometimes older children benefit from an acronym, or an abbreviation, made from the letters of a word. For example, take the word *stress*. You and your child could come up with your own acronym using each letter in the word to remind your child of the approach to take when faced with a potentially stressful situation. An example is:

Say to self, "I can handle this" and keep anxiety away while I

Think of strategies,

Opt for the best solution, and

Put my plan in place and remember to keep it all in perspective.

MINDSET

Carol Dweck of Stanford University has written extensively on the importance of having a *growth mindset* as opposed to a *fixed mindset*. In her book, *Mindset: The New Psychology of Success* (2006), she explained that a person with a *growth mindset* believes basic qualities are not fixed but can be cultivated through efforts. In contrast, a person with a *fixed mindset* believes that performance is a reflection of intelligence and is fixed (pp. 6–7). Her three decades of research have shown that students with a growth mindset made better grades because they "mobilized their resources for learning" (p. 58) by putting forth more effort because they believed it would make a difference than those with a fixed mindset: "The fixed mindset limits achievement. It fills people's minds with interfering thoughts, it makes effort disagreeable, and it leads to inferior learning strategies" (p. 67).

If a child has a *growth mindset*, more than likely he will be able to:

O accept reality and not waste time and energy dwelling in the past,

O face fears because he will have confidence that he has the resources to cope with a situation or will be able to seek assistance when necessary, and

O establish goals that help him to move forward and be proactive.

RESOURCES

Mindsets for Parents: Strategies to Encourage Growth Mindsets in Kids by Mary Cay Ricci and Margaret Lee provides tools and strategies for creating a growth mindset home environment.

The Most Magnificent Thing by Ashley Spires (ages 3–7) shows the rewards of perseverance as a girl tries to create her "magnificent" thing.

Your Fantastic Elastic Brain: Stretch It, Shape It by JoAnn Deak and Sarah Ackerley (ages 4–8) helps children understand how trying new things and overcoming fears can actually strengthen your brain.

Everyone Can Learn to Ride a Bicycle by Chris Raschka (ages 4–8) takes the reader on the journey of a young girl as she goes through the ups and downs of learning and finally succeeding to ride a bicycle.

NURTURING ENVIRONMENT

It is not surprising that children exposed to conflict and tension absorb that negativity and stress. In today's fast-paced, frenetic world, a child needs some refuge. If the family can serve that role, the child is much better equipped to meet the demands of society. Ideally, the family is a place where a child can learn mutual respect, how to be a team player, and how to care for and support others. Strong family bonds give a child a sense of identity and decrease feelings of isolation. We have all experienced the stress-relieving quality of a warm hug from a family member.

A key part of having a nurturing environment is having time to talk and *really listen* to your child. Children can be a wealth of information if we stop what we are doing and make them feel important enough to tell us what is going on in their lives. Helping them problem solve a troubling situation can be very empowering to them, teach them problem-solving skills, and improve your relationship all at the same time.

CONVERSATION STARTER
DISCUSSING THE SCHOOL DAY

Try to set aside some time every day to talk to your child about the school day. If she is reluctant to share, try asking her to rate the day on a scale of 1 to 10, with 10 being the best. If that doesn't generate much conversation, try asking her to rate different aspects of the day from 1 to 10 like lunch, recess, math class, etc.

It is important to try to remember the names of the children discussed. Friendships frequently change. Peer relationships, and especially the lack of them, can be a great source of stress for your child. Through these discussions, you can help your child figure out which characteristics in other children lead to good friendships. As children become older, you can help them understand other children's motives and actions. When your child is discussing classmates, it is important to remember there are always two sides to every story. Your goal is to help your child maintain positive peer relations, so be careful of negative comments about classmates. As we have said before, if you feel your child is being bullied, do not hesitate to contact the teacher and/or the principal.

RESOURCES

How to Talk So Kids Will Listen & Listen So Kids Will Talk by Adele Faber and Elaine Mazlish includes suggestions on opening up lines of communication with your child.

The Gentle Art of Communicating With Kids by Suzette Haden Elgin helps parents learn techniques to talk to their children positively and productively.

Aha! Parenting (http://www.ahaparenting.com) offers articles about communicating with children of all ages.

ACTIVITY
CREATE A COPING KIT

Work with your child to create a "coping kit" to use when stressed. Both you and your child could have your own kit that contains things that help each of you get a handle on the stress you are experiencing. Your kit might contain headphones, inspirational quotations, journaling material, or mementos that bring wonderful memories. For example, your child's kit may contain:

- ☐ small toys;

- ☐ pictures of family, friends, or favorite vacations;

- ☐ crayons and small pieces of paper; or

- ☐ a squishy ball or small stuffed animal.

If your child is older and doesn't need concrete items, help him or her make a list of strategies to turn to when stressed or anxious. Let him or her use creativity and problem-solving skills to decide how it should look, what strategies to include, and where it should be placed.

CHAPTER 10

Yoga, Mindfulness, and Meditation

Nothing can bring you peace but yourself.
—Ralph Waldo Emerson

> **KEY POINT:** Activities focusing on breathing can connect the body to the nervous system and interrupt unwanted, stressful thoughts.
>
> **THINKING POINT:** Could both my child and I benefit from yoga?

Activities focusing on breathing and being in the present, including yoga, meditation, mindfulness, and tai chi, provide links to the nervous system and can promote well-being. "Brain breaks" or some form of breathing and physical activity are also becoming increasingly important and are a part of the daily routine in many schools.

BREATHING

In yoga, mindfulness, and meditation, breath control is one of the key factors in helping participants gain better control over their thoughts. If your child is a worrier who obsesses about certain thoughts, learning to count full, deep breaths can interrupt the obsessions and unwanted thoughts. Breathing connects the body to the nervous system, a key in stress control.

There are many techniques for breath control. The key will be finding one that your child thinks will be a helpful tool and is willing to use.
Encourage your child to use deep, diaphragmatic breathing where he is
inhaling and exhaling deeply. Some of the most popular ones involve
having your child:

O breathe in to the count of 3–5 and breathe out to the count of
3–5;

O lie on the floor with his hands on his stomach and feel his belly
expand as breaths are taken in and out—sometimes it is helpful
to visualize blowing up a balloon and then letting the air out of
it;

O pretend to blow out birthday candles;

O imagine blowing on a feather, sending it up above the head and
watching it float back down; or

O push the palms of his hands together while breathing in to the
count of 3–5 and breathe out.

RESOURCES

*Sea Otter Cove: Introducing Relaxation Breathing to Lower Anxiety, Decrease
Stress and Control Anger While Promoting Peaceful Sleep* by Lori Lite
(ages 6–12) teaches children breathing techniques.

Breathe2Relax (older children and adults) is a stress management app
with practice exercises for diaphragmatic breathing.

YOGA

Yoga has gone mainstream. Even NFL teams are having their members do yoga on a routine basis, and some schools incorporate it into their
day. Yoga in its simplest form entails a series of movements that encourage stretching with specific poses, many of which should be familiar, such
as "downward dog" and "tree."

Many recreation centers and gyms have yoga classes targeted for children. If you can't access an organized class, try instructional yoga videos
for children. Many children that we know enjoy doing yoga at home
with their parents, either from an instructional video or from the parent

leading the yoga movements. Creating a special time for you and your child may be difficult but can produce so many positive results in terms of opening communication, fostering positive relationships, and teaching new skills.

RESOURCES

I Am Yoga by Susan Verde (ages 4–8) encourages kids to explore yoga and includes a guide to 16 yoga poses.

Good Night Yoga: A Pose-by-Pose Bedtime Story by Mariam Gates (ages 4–8) features yoga poses to relax the body and mind and improve sleep.

Angel Bear Yoga by Christi Eley and Mark Eley is a parent-child yoga program that includes lesson books, yoga pose playing cards, and CDs.

Yoga Pretzels by Tara Guber and Leah Kalish is a set of 50 yoga pose cards for kids and parents.

MINDFULNESS AND MEDITATION

For the record, *mindfulness* and *meditation* are often used interchangeably, but they are not exactly the same. Mindfulness involves paying attention to the present in a nonjudgmental way. Meditation involves taking yourself out of your environment by focusing on a single thought or object, ultimately leading to a higher consciousness. Mindfulness is considered to be a meditation practice. Research supports mindfulness and meditation as effective tools to help children handle worry and anxiety because they take the attention away from the worries and help children get in touch with and accept emotions without judgment. They can also be quite helpful to parents by helping parents be more aware of their emotions and choose responses more carefully and thoughtfully.

Actress Goldie Hawn developed a strong interest in helping children deal with stress and anxiety through mindfulness and meditation. Through the Hawn Foundation, she asked a team of educators, neurologists, psychologists, and social scientists to develop a new curriculum that involves lessons on how the brain works and incorporates social-emotional development and metacognition—thinking about thinking—

through meditation (Wickelgren, 2011). It is called MindUP and it is currently being successfully implemented in a number of schools.

When beginning mindfulness activities, it is important to remember that children are still very concrete, so often using an object as a visual for focusing their senses, such as by listening to a bell, is a good way to start. Keep in mind their attention span, which may vary from 1 to 5 minutes. Having an environment as calm and quiet as possible is also important. As with anything else you try to teach your child, you will be more successful at it if you have actually tried it first.

Rick Presta (2016) suggested introducing 4 to 6 year olds to mindfulness by getting them to pay attention to their five senses. He suggests "asking them to stop whatever they are doing and thinking and really pay attention to the world around them." For 7 to 12 year olds he recommends introducing "the concept of paying attention, being balanced and having compassion into the mindfulness mix" (2016).

MINDFULNESS ACTIVITIES

O Have your child observe a small piece of food, such as popcorn, a cracker, or a raisin. Hooker and Fodor (2008) suggested guiding your child to observe the food as if seeing it for the first time. Have your child note the texture, color, smell, and ultimately put it in his mouth and notice the actual taste of the food. (The raisin meditation is a classic. There are scripts and even YouTube videos available online.)

O Ring a bell or use a phone app that has a consistent sound. Tell your child to keep listening to the sound until she can no longer hear it.

O Go on nature walks through the neighborhood and ask your child to observe things he hasn't noticed before.

O If you are more comfortable using guided mindfulness activities for children read by someone else, access recorded exercises at http://annakaharris.com/mindfulness-for-children.

RESOURCES

Visiting Feelings by Lauren Rubenstein (ages 4–8) encourages mindfulness and awareness.

1-2-3 A Calmer Me: Helping Children Cope When Emotions Get Out of Control by Colleen A. Patterson and Brenda S. Miles (ages 4–8) introduces children to a rhyming mantra.

Silence by Lemniscates (ages 4–8) has children reflect on their feelings and develop mindfulness.

Sitting Still Like a Frog: Mindfulness Exercises for Kids (and Their Parents) by Eline Snel (ages 5 and up) contains mindfulness exercises and an accompanying audio CD with guided meditations.

Planting Seeds: Practicing Mindfulness With Children by Thich Nhat Hanh and the Plum Village Community (ages 5 and up) also contains a CD with meditations and fun activities for encouraging mindfulness.

Take the Time: Mindfulness for Kids by Maud Roegiers (ages 6–8) encourages self-awareness and mindfulness.

Mind Over Basketball: Coach Yourself to Handle Stress by Jane Weierbach and Elizabeth Phillips-Hershey (ages 8–11) features exercises to build confidence to help children coach themselves through worry and stress.

MEDITATION

Meditations for children often involve guided imagery with a goal of helping children calm their thinking and find the strength and wisdom within themselves. The goal is to help children visualize themselves in a calm space where they can nonjudgmentally think about their feelings and thoughts and then let them go as they come back to a place of calmness. You may find it calming to make up meditations for your child, read scripted ones, or play them on YouTube or iTunes. A sample meditation is as follows:

Imagine yourself in a quiet place lying under a large tree with big, leafy branches. Take in a deep breath and quietly breathe it out. Listen to the wind rustling the leaves and watch as they are blown to and fro and sparkle in the sunlight. Feel the cool breeze caused by the branches moving in the wind. Look closely to see if there are any flowers or acorns on the tree. Watch carefully for any birds or squirrels who may find comfort and safety in the boughs of the tree. Think of this tree as your special place where you can completely relax and possibly even close your eyes and fall asleep. You can come to this place often and think about your day and let anything that is bothering you be taken up by the cool breeze of the branches and let it float away into the sky, never to bother you again. When you are ready, quietly leave the tree. With a deep breath in and out, go on with your day.

RESOURCES

Meditation Is an Open Sky: Mindfulness for Kids by Whitney Stewart (ages 7–10) teaches children simple exercises to develop meditation and mindfulness skills.

Teaching Mindfulness to Children by Karen E. Hooker and Iris E. Fodor includes an example of a guided meditation (available at http://www. gisc.org/gestaltreview/documents/teachingmindfulnesstochildren.pdf).

"Spider-Man: Practicing Mindfulness and Increasing Focus" by Kids Relaxation is a superhero-themed script (available at http://kids relaxation.com/uncategorized/spider-man-practicing-mindfulness-and-increasing-focus).

"Hot Air Balloon Ride: A Guided Meditation for Kids, Children's Visualization for Sleep and Dreaming" by Amelia Schmelzer is an example of one of the many children's meditations available on YouTube (available at https://www.youtube.com/watch?v=vlv6Y1tq1sQ).

Guided Meditation for Primary Students by BuddhaNet includes scripts for guided meditations (available at http://www.buddhanet.net/pdf_file/med-guided2.pdf).

Sleep Meditations for Kids by Christiane Kerr (ages 4–12) is an app that features calming bedtime relaxation stories for children.

My Light Shines Bright (ages 8–12) is an app that features 32 guided meditations.

Meditation Studio by Gaiam is an app, which provides meditations with special collections for kids, teens, and moms.

CHAPTER 11

Seeking a Happy, Balanced Life

Stressed spelled backwards is desserts.

—Loretta LaRoche

KEY POINTS:

O Outside interests, often considered hobbies or passions, help a child return to equilibrium when stressed.

O Religion or spirituality can foster a sense of purpose and meaning and decrease feelings of isolation.

O A balanced life covers all the bases—physical activity, good nutrition, adequate rest, and downtime for relaxation. Make sure your child has time for activities that nurture his or her spirit and creativity.

THINKING POINT: Does my child have activities that help him or her relax? If not, what can I do to help him or her discover them?

OUTSIDE INTERESTS

When we have activities that allow us to "lose ourselves" and become completely immersed in the activity, we can lose track of time and often develop a sense of calm. These activities are usually passions or hobbies. Helping your child find and develop these kinds of activities can be invaluable to mental health. They allow him to take a mini-break from life. Sometimes, even very young children, can recognize which activities are calming for them. Parents were working with 5-year-old Madeline to help her reduce her tantrums and gain better self-control. It happened that going to a local art studio where she painted ceramic figures was a favorite and engrossing activity for her. One day she was denied her own way, and as she began to wail, she said, "I want to go to Plaster Fun Time." It was almost as if she recognized that as a calming place for her where she felt totally in control.

Interests can be in the arts, sports, social arena, reading, or just having quiet time. Parents often ask about video games. True, many children are very passionate about gaming and can spend countless hours in front of the computer. As a parent, you will have to decide if this truly brings your child back to equilibrium when he is upset or if it agitates him or causes a ruckus when he must sign off the game. Television can be viewed the same way. It can be fine in moderation and if you are aware of the programming.

Some parents of older elementary children tell us their children don't have any passions. Our tip: Don't stop searching. There are countless things out there and you never know when something may capture your child's interest and become an important stress reliever. Summertime is a great time for kids to explore different activities through camps and travel. Expose them to books on different subjects and people with various interests. Model in your own life how activities you are passionate about enhance your life.

STRATEGIES TO HELP YOUR CHILD DEVELOP INTERESTS

Provide downtime. It goes without saying that in order to pursue an interest or quiet time, you must make sure your child has enough downtime in his or her schedule to pursue those activities. This can be difficult if your child is in aftercare until 6 p.m. and then has dinner and homework. If it can't happen before bedtime, try to make sure there is time on the weekends for those activities that nurture your child's spirit

Don't forget time for some fun. If time permits, try to have one mood-elevating activity per day depending on your child's interests. It could be something as simple as throwing a ball back and forth or something as involved as a multistep craft project.

Plan special events. Plan in advance for special events to give your child the joy of anticipation.

RESOURCES

"Mining for Gold: Helping Your Children Discover Their Passion" by Jan DeLisle includes tips for parents to help find their children's passions (available at http://sengifted.org/mining-for-gold-helping-your-child-discover-their-passion).

Incredible You! 10 Ways to Let Your Greatness Shine Through by Wayne W. Dyer and Kristina Tracy (ages 4–9) seeks to help children discover their unique gifts.

RELIGION AND SPIRITUALITY

Believing in a higher power can help give children a perspective about the world and encourages them to focus on the needs of others rather than themselves. Often a church, synagogue, or other religious community is a nurturing, caring group that provides a safety net for children and their families. Believing in a higher power helps alleviate some of the stress caused by the chaos and calamities of the world. The values taught by many religions reinforce the concept of gratefulness and contribute to happy, balanced, and productive lives.

Dez, the parent of Hannah, explained:

When you have faith you are able to get a bigger, better perspective of what truly matters. Find peace by focusing on daily praising, praying, and pondering what God's plan is for your child's life instead of sadness, struggles, and stress in the world. You'll go from looking at the problem right in front of you to anticipating and claiming the goodness of God's promises. If you allow stress to take over your life, it will with fatal consequences to your child and entire family. That's where faith is vital to conquering the daily stressors. Continue to remind your child to tilt her head up to heaven and look at the big picture instead of staring at what is right in front of her.

You and God make a majority, so when things get tough, teach your child to silently pray for His strength. This will help your child understand he or she is not alone in dealing with stressful circumstances and that today's troubles could be tomorrow's triumphs.

RESOURCES

Grace for the Moment: 365 Devotions for Kids by Max Lucado (ages 6–10) is for older children to read independently or younger children to read with an adult.

Thank You, God! A Jewish Child's Book of Prayers by Judyth Groner and Madeline Wikler (ages 4–7) contains 21 simple prayers in Hebrew and English.

The Purpose Driven Life Devotional for Kids by Rick Warren (ages 8–12) is based on the best-selling adult book.

BALANCED LIFE

Good nutrition is essential for everyday functioning and especially important in stress management. Vitamins considered to play a role include Vitamin C, found in citrus and green leafy vegetables; Vitamin B, found in whole grains, eggs, nuts, beans, and meat; and Vitamin A, found in meat, carrots, and eggs. Eating a balanced diet with moderate servings and few processed foods is key. Involve children in the grocery shopping, meal planning, and cooking to perk up their appetites and interest in food. Sometimes it is a big challenge to get children to eat healthy but something you shouldn't give up on because it has major implications on their health and well-being now and in the future.

Exercise plays a very important role in stress management. The American Academy of Pediatrics (2015) recommends that children over 6 years of age have at least 60 minutes of physical activity every day for their general well-being. It doesn't have to be done all at once but can be broken up into segments. If you have difficulty getting your children up and off the couch, work with them to set a fitness goal, and then make a daily chart that shows what they will do each day to meet that goal. Reward them with praise and special opportunities for working toward the goal.

Adults know all too well that the amount and quality of their sleep impacts their stress management capabilities. All parents know that is especially true for children, as we have probably all dealt with tired children's meltdowns. The American Academy of Pediatrics (2016) recommended that children ages 3–5 should sleep 10–13 hours, and children ages 6–12 should sleep 9–12 hours in a 24-hour period. If your child has trouble falling asleep, make sure you eliminate screen time at least a half an hour before bedtime, provide a calm bedtime routine, and don't allow devices and screens in the bedroom. Many parents we know have success with having all devices stay on a central charging station overnight.

ACTIVITIES FOR ENCOURAGING HEALTHY EATING

Encourage familiarity with the food pyramid. If you enter "food pyramid" in a search engine, you will find many examples you can print. Websites to help you and your children include ChooseMyPlate. gov (https://www.choosemyplate.gov/kids), which features games and activities.

Help young children identify food groups. If you have play or pretend food in your house, let your child sort the foods into the different food groups. If you do not, use pictures of foods cut from magazines or printed from the Internet.

ACTIVITIES FOR ENCOURAGING PHYSICAL ACTIVITY

Create your own activities. Jumping rope, playing hopscotch, running relay races, and participating in Red Rover and Simon Says are all ways to increase physical activity with minimal props.

Move like an animal. "Move Like an Animal Cards" are printable cards that instruct children to move in the way the pictured animal might move. They are available for $3.00 through Teachers Pay Teachers (https://www.teacherspayteachers.com/Product/Move-Like-an-Animal-Cards-1139499).

Play paper bag kick ball. Stock Kranowitz (2016) advises parents to take a paper bag and scrunch it tightly into a ball. Your child can kick it around the yard repeatedly and safely (p. 19).

Play copy cat. Ask your child to watch and copy what you do. Move parts of your body in various ways, such as raising your hand over your head or balancing on one foot and wiggling the other foot in the air. Then, ask your child to lead while you copy (Stock Kranowitz, p. 20).

RESOURCES

The Busy Body Book: A Kid's Guide to Fitness by Lizzy Rockwell (ages 3–7) includes information about how the body works and the importance of physical activity.

Good Enough to Eat: A Kid's Guide to Food and Nutrition by Lizzy Rockwell (ages 4–8) teaches children about the nutrient groups, digestion, and calories, and includes kid-friendly recipes.

Why Should I Eat Well? by Claire Llewellyn (ages 4–8) helps kids understand the importance of good eating habits.

Kid Chef: The Foodie Kids Cookbook: Healthy Recipes and Culinary Skills for the New Cook in the Kitchen by Melina Hammer (ages 8–13) is an easy-to-follow cookbook that includes sections on a variety of culinary skills for beginners in the kitchen.

Conclusion

We wish you the best as you and your child strive to develop positive and productive ways to cope with stress, which seems to be a constant in our society. You've read a lot of information, and as long as you are intentional in applying what you learned, your child will be better off. Remember that stress can be situational or more long term, but both are manageable. Handled appropriately, stress can be a motivating factor in your child's life, but if constant and unrelenting, it can lead to anxiety, depression, and physical problems. Coping strategies including open communication, a balanced lifestyle, and a growth mindset can help foster the resilience your child needs. Identify your child's stress level and apply some of the tools you've learned about from these chapters.

We live in times where people want things quickly, but changing the way a child copes with stress takes time. Some families we work with want to stop trying before they've given the stress tool enough time to become effective. Families then say, "We've tried everything and nothing worked." This is true because they sampled everything but never grasped anything. The most effective stress-busting families identify a variety of tools and apply them consistently. This is our hope for you!

Resources
for Parents

BOOKS

The Gentle Art of Communicating With Kids by Suzette Haden Elgin helps parents learn techniques to talk to their children positively and productively.

How to Talk So Kids Will Listen & Listen So Kids Will Talk by Adele Faber and Elaine Mazlish includes suggestions on opening up lines of communication with your child.

Kids Who Laugh: How to Develop Your Child's Sense of Humor by Louis R. Franzini examines the humor and gives parents suggestions to help their child with laughter.

Mindsets for Parents: Strategies to Encourage Growth Mindsets in Kids by Mary Cay Ricci and Margaret Lee provides tools and strategies for creating a growth mindset home environment.

WEBSITES

Aha! Parenting (http://www.ahaparenting.com) offers articles about communicating with children of all ages.

"Mining for Gold: Helping Your Children Discover Their Passion" by Jan DeLisle includes tips for parents to help find their children's passions (available at http://sengifted.org/mining-for-gold-helping-your-child-discover-their-passion).

Resources for Kids

BOOKS

LEARNING ABOUT STRESS, ANXIETY, AND FEELINGS

How Are You Peeling? by Saxton Freymann and Joost Elffers (ages 4–8) features fruits and vegetables with various expressions to spark discussions of feelings for young children.

I'm Frustrated (Dealing With Feelings) by Elizabeth Crary (ages 3–8) depicts situations that require coping skills and allows readers to choose their own endings.

Double-Dip Feelings: Stories to Help Children Understand Emotions (2nd ed.) by Barbara S. Cain (ages 4–8) helps children with the experience of having contrasting feelings at the same time.

Feelings by Aliki (ages 4–8) features many visuals of different emotions.

Max Archer, Kid Detective: The Case of the Recurring Stomachaches by Howard J. Bennett (ages 7–9) is written by a pediatrician.

My Book Full of Feelings: How to Control and React to the Size of Your Emotions: An Interactive Workbook for Parents, Professionals and Children by Amy V. Jaffe and Luci Gardner helps children identify the intensity of emotions and respond appropriately. It is reusable and includes a dry erase marker so you can add situations unique to your child.

Shy Spaghetti and Excited Eggs: A Kid's Menu of Feelings by Marc Nemiroff and Jane Annunziata (ages 4–8) helps children identify their emotions.

Ten Turtles on Tuesday: A Story for Children About Obsessive-Compulsive Disorder by Ellen Flanagan Burns (ages 8–12) is about a child who learns to handle anxious thoughts and compulsions with the help of her family and her therapist.

Understanding Myself: A Kid's Guide to Intense Emotions and Strong Feelings by Mary C. Lamia (ages 8–13) helps children with strategies for handling emotions.

The Way I Feel by Janan Cain (ages 3–8) helps children understand various emotions.

OVERCOMING FEAR AND WORRY

Don't Put Yourself Down in Circus Town: A Story About Self-Confidence by Frank J. Sileo (ages 6–10) highlights circus performers and their ringmaster as they learn to bounce back from mistakes and fear, learning to feel more confident in the process.

Is a Worry Worrying You? by Ferida Wolff (ages 4–8) stresses understanding worries and using creative problem solving.

Sometimes I'm Scared by Jane Annunziata (ages 5–8) discusses common fears through children's eyes and how they can deal with them to get back to being kids again.

What to Do When You Worry Too Much: A Kid's Guide to Overcoming Anxiety by Dawn Huebner (ages 6–12) is an interactive self-help book that uses CBT techniques.

When Fuzzy Was Afraid of Big and Loud Things by Inger Maier (ages 2–4) depicts Fuzzy the sheep dealing with common fears.

When Lizzy Was Afraid of Trying New Things by Inger Maier (ages 2–4) features Fuzzy's little sister, Lizzy, who is afraid of making mistakes.

Woe Is Me: The Wild Adventures of Woe the Worried by Matt Casper (ages 7–12) is a chapter book and part of the Emotes series, which includes small characters that can be purchased separately (available at https://www.creativetherapystore.com).

OVERCOMING PERFECTIONISM

The Girl Who Never Made Mistakes by Mark Pett and Gary Rubinstein (ages 4–8*)* features a 9-year-old girl who makes her first mistake in a very public way.

What to Do When Mistakes Make You Quake: A Kid's Guide to Accepting Imperfection by Claire A. B. Freeland and Jacqueline B. Toner (ages 6–12) aims to help children who are too hard on themselves.

Nobody's Perfect: A Story for Children About Perfectionism by Ellen Flanagan Burns (ages 8–12) is about a child who learns not to be so concerned about being the best.

STRESS AT SCHOOL

General Academic Pressures:

Annie's Plan: Taking Charge of Schoolwork and Homework by Jeanne Kraus (ages 4–8) shows a girl establishing a plan to improve her organizational and study skills.

Sam and Gram and the First Day of School by Dianne Blomberg (ages 4–6) takes readers through a typical first day of school.

School Made Easier: A Kid's Guide to Study Strategies and Anxiety-Busting Tools by Wendy L. Moss and Robin Deluca-Acconi (ages 10–13) teaches students how to avoid being overwhelmed so they can reduce their anxiety and improve school-related skills.

Stickley Sticks to It!: A Frog's Guide to Getting Things Done by Brenda S. Miles (ages 4–8) shows children how to persevere until a job is finished.

Resistance to Go to School:

Oh No, School! by Hae-Kyung Chang (ages 4–7) is a story about a young girl who does not want to go to school but is encouraged by her mother to think differently about the things she doesn't like about school.

Social Pressures:

Blue Cheese Breath and Stinky Feet: How to Deal with Bullies by Catherine DePino (ages 6–12) involves parents helping a student devise plans for dealing with a school bully.

Boss No More by Estelle Meens (ages 4–8) depicts the results of always wanting to be in charge.

Circle of Three: Enough Friendship to Go Around? by Elizabeth Brokamp (ages 8–12) features three girls who are best friends but have their ups and downs.

Dealing With Bullies by Pam Scheunemann (ages 4–6) contains full glossy pictures appropriate for younger children.

Friends Always by Tanja Wenisch (ages 4–8) shows the vacillation of children's friendships between fighting and making up.

I Don't Know Why . . . I Guess I'm Shy: Taming Imaginary Fears by Barbara Cain (ages 4–8) shows children that being shy doesn't have to limit fun and friendships.

I'm Like You, You're Like Me: A Child's Book About Understanding and Celebrating Each Other by Cindy Gainer (ages 4–8) helps children discover differences.

It's Mine! by Leo Lionni (ages 3–7) features three funny frogs who learn to share.

Martha Doesn't Share! by Samantha Berger (ages 4–8) helps Martha learn that when you don't share, you play alone.

Nobody Likes Me, Everybody Hates Me: The Top 25 Friendship Problems and How to Solve Them by Michele Borba is a book for parents about teaching children friendship-building skills.

Sally Sore Loser: A Story About Winning and Losing by Frank J. Sileo (ages 4–8) is about helping a child learn to value having fun over winning and losing.

Toodles and Teeny: A Story About Friendship by Jill Neimark and Marcella Bakur Weiner (ages 4–8) features friendship in the making.

STRESS IN THE COMMUNITY

Going to the Dentist:

The Berenstain Bears Visit the Dentist by Stan Berenstain and Jan Berenstain (ages 3–7) is a classic book for helping calm kids' fears of going to the dentist.

Curious George Visits the Dentist by H. A. Rey (ages 4–7) helps children learn about dental hygiene and going to the dentist.

Going to the Dentist by Anne Civardi (ages 3+) helps explain the first trip to a dentist.

Just Going to the Dentist by Mercer Mayer (ages 3–7) helps kids learn going to the dentist is not so bad.

Going to the Dentist by Anne Civardi (ages 3+) helps explain the first trip to a dentist.

Going to the Doctor:

The Berenstain Bears Go to the Doctor by Stan Berenstain and Jan Berenstain (ages 3–7) is a classic book to teach children what happens when they go to the doctor.

Franklin Goes to the Hospital by Paulette Bourgeois (ages 3–8) helps children know when they are scared they can still feel brave.

Lions Aren't Scared of Shots by Howard J. Bennett (ages 8–12) helps children deal with the fear of getting a shot.

Say Ahhh!: Dora Goes to the Doctor by Phoebe Beinstein (ages 3–7) helps children understand going to the doctor.

Fear of Sleeping Alone:

I Love to Sleep in My Own Bed by Shelley Admont (ages 2–7) is Jimmy the bunny's adventure for learning to sleep alone.

I Sleep in My Own Bed by Glenn Wright (ages 4+) deals with the fear of sleeping in bed alone or having a bad dream.

Mommy, I Want to Sleep in Your Bed! by Harriet Ziefert (ages 3–7) explains how Charlie learns to sleep alone.

Night Light: A Story for Children Afraid of the Dark by Jack Dutro (ages 4–9) depicts how Kalispel learns to face his fear of daylight.

Scary Night Visitors: A Story for Children With Bedtime Fears by Irene Wineman Marcus and Paul Marcus (ages 4–8) helps parents and children handle bedtime fears.

Monster Fear:

The Berenstain Bears and the Bad Dream by Stan Berenstain and Jan Berenstain (ages 3–7) teaches children that dreams can be scary but are not real.

The Berenstain Bears in the Dark by Stan Berenstain and Jan Berenstain (fear of the dark; ages 3–7) is a classic book for teaching children how to overcome fears.

Franklin in the Dark by Paulette Bourgeois (fear of the dark; ages 3–8) helps children learn how to come out of their shell.

There's a Nightmare in My Closet by Mercer Mayer (ages 3–5) is a classic for helping children understand nightmares.

STRESS IN THE FAMILY

Divorce:

I Am Living in 2 Homes by Garcelle Beauvais (ages 4–7) follows twins as they learn the benefits of having two homes.

It's Not Your Fault, Koko Bear by Vicki Lansky (ages 3–7) is a story about a loveable bear who doesn't want two homes but learns how to make the best of it.

My Family's Changing by Pat Thomas (ages 4–7) also includes questions to help children process what they are going through.

Two Homes by Claire Masurel (ages 3–7) follows Alex's journey of setting up special features at each parent's home.

When Mom and Dad Divorce by Emily Menendez-Aponte (ages 8–12) helps children deal with the emotions they experience during divorce.

A New Baby:

The Berenstain Bears' New Baby by Stan Berenstain and Jan Berenstain (ages 3–7) helps children adjust to new life with a baby.

The Berenstain Bears and Baby Makes Five by Stan Berenstain and Jan Berenstain (ages 3–7) depicts adjustments siblings make when Honey the baby comes and wants all of the attention.

Big Brother Now: A Story About Me and Our New Baby by Annette Sheldon (ages 2–5) demonstrates how children can still feel loved moving from being an only child to a big brother.

Big Sister Now: A Story About Me and Our New Baby by Annette Sheldon (ages 2–5) features Kate's feelings about welcoming a baby brother.

Elana's Ears, or How I Became the Best Big Sister in the World by Gloria Roth Lowell (ages 3–8) features a girl adjusting to being a big sister who learns her baby sister can't hear.

The New Baby by Mercer Mayer (ages 3–7) follows Little Critter's adjustment to a new sibling.

Moving:

Big Ernie's New Home: A Story for Young Children Who Are Moving by Teresa Martin and Whitney Martin (ages 2–5) follows children's feelings of anxiety and sadness during a move.

Boomer's Big Day by Constance W. McGeorge (ages 3–6) helps children explore their feelings of confusion and concern on moving day.

My Very Exciting, Sorta Scary, Big Move: A Workbook for Children Moving to a New Home by Lori Attanasio Woodring (ages 5–11) is a workbook that walks children through the steps of moving.

Death of a Family Member or Relative:

I'll Always Love You by Hans Wilhelm (ages 3–7) follows a boy when his dog, Elfie, dies.

I Miss You: A First Look at Death by Pat Thomas (ages 4–8) helps children deal with feelings experienced when someone close to them dies.

Sad Isn't Bad: A Good-Grief Guidebook for Kids Dealing With Loss by Michaelene Mundy (ages 4–8) contains positive affirmations to help children deal with loss.

Terminal Illness:

Help Me Say Goodbye: Activities for Helping Kids Cope When a Special Person Dies by Janis Silverman (ages 3+) is for kids whose family member is sick or dies.

Where Did Mommy's Superpowers Go? by Jenifer Gershman (ages 3+) helps children understand cancer.

STRESS BUSTERS

Resiliency:

Bounce Back: How to Be a Resilient Kid by Wendy L. Moss (ages 8–12) builds resiliency skills.

The Hugging Tree: A Story About Resilience by Jill Neimark (ages 5–8) teaches children about hope and resilience.

What Do You Do With a Problem? by Kobi Yamada (ages 4–8) encourages seeing the possibilities in problems.

Optimism:

Be Positive!: A Book About Optimism by Cheri J. Meiners (ages 4–8) helps children discover how choices they make can lead to happiness and feeling capable.

Did I Ever Tell You How Lucky You Are? by Dr. Seuss (ages 5–9) features Dr. Seuss's optimism.

How Full Is Your Bucket? For Kids by Tom Rath and Mary Rekmeyer (ages 3–8) introduces the concept of creating happiness by doing nice things for others.

How to Get Unstuck From the Negative Muck: A Kid's Guide to Getting Rid of Negative Thinking by Lake Sullivan presents cognitive behavioral therapy strategies and includes journal exercises for kids.

I Think, I Am!: Teaching Kids the Power of Affirmations by Louise Hay and Kristina Tracy (ages 3–7) helps children realize that their thoughts play a powerful role in what happens in their lives.

What to Do When You Grumble Too Much: A Kid's Guide to Overcoming Negativity by Dawn Huebner (ages 6–12) shows children different ways to respond to life's ups and downs.

Sense of Humor:

The Book With No Pictures by B. J. Novak (ages 5–8) is a funny book with silly made-up words that the person reading the book has to read aloud.

The Day the Crayons Quit by Drew Daywalt (ages 3–7) features Duncan, a young boy who gets creative letters from his crayons.

Just Joking: 300 Hilarious Jokes, Tricky Tongue Twisters, and Ridiculous Riddles by National Geographic Kids (ages 7–10) features tongue twisters, riddles, and jokes.

Laugh-Out-Loud Jokes for Kids by Rob Elliott (ages 7–10) features jokes children enjoy.

Scholastic Reader Level 1: Get the Giggles: A First Joke Book by Bronwen Davies (ages 4–7) has multiple jokes to be enjoyed by all.

Mindset:

Everyone Can Learn to Ride a Bicycle by Chris Raschka (ages 4–8) takes the reader on the journey of a young girl as she goes through the ups and downs of learning and finally succeeding to ride a bicycle.

The Most Magnificent Thing by Ashley Spires (ages 3–7) shows the rewards of perseverance as a girl tries to create her "magnificent" thing.

Your Fantastic Elastic Brain: Stretch It, Shape It by JoAnn Deak and Sarah Ackerley (ages 4–8) helps children understand how trying new things and overcoming fears can actually strengthen your brain.

Yoga:

I Am Yoga by Susan Verde (ages 4–8) encourages kids to explore yoga and includes a guide to 16 yoga poses.

Good Night Yoga: A Pose-by-Pose Bedtime Story by Mariam Gates (ages 4–8) features yoga poses to relax the body and mind and improve sleep.

Mindfulness and Meditation:

1-2-3 A Calmer Me: Helping Children Cope When Emotions Get Out of Control by Colleen A. Patterson and Brenda S. Miles (ages 4–8) introduces children to a rhyming mantra.

Master of Mindfulness: How to Be Your Own Superhero in Times of Stress by Laurie Grossman (ages 5–12) provides strategies by kids, for kids to use in times of stress.

Meditation Is an Open Sky: Mindfulness for Kids by Whitney Stewart (ages 7–10) teaches children simple exercises to develop meditation and mindfulness skills.

Mind Over Basketball: Coach Yourself to Handle Stress by Jane Weierbach and Elizabeth Phillips-Hershey (ages 8–11) features exercises to build confidence to help children coach themselves through worry and stress.

Planting Seeds: Practicing Mindfulness With Children by Thich Nhat Hanh and the Plum Village Community (ages 5 and up) also contains a CD with meditations and fun activities for encouraging mindfulness.

Puppy Mind by Andrew Jordan Nance (ages 3–7) features a young boy whose mind wanders, and he learns to control it through breathing and thought.

Sea Otter Cove: Introducing Relaxation Breathing to Lower Anxiety, Decrease Stress and Control Anger While Promoting Peaceful Sleep by Lori Lite (ages 6–12) teaches children breathing techniques.

Silence by Lemniscates (ages 4–8) has children reflect on their feelings and develop mindfulness.

Sitting Still Like a Frog: Mindfulness Exercises for Kids (and Their Parents) by Eline Snel (ages 5 and up) contains mindfulness exercises and an accompanying audio CD with guided meditations.

Take the Time: Mindfulness for Kids by Maud Roegiers (ages 6–8) encourages self-awareness and mindfulness.

Visiting Feelings by Lauren Rubenstein (ages 4–8) encourages mindfulness and awareness.

Outside Interests:

Incredible You! 10 Ways to Let Your Greatness Shine Through by Wayne W. Dyer and Kristina Tracy (ages 4–9) seeks to help children discover their unique gifts.

Religion and Spirituality:

Grace for the Moment: 365 Devotions for Kids by Max Lucado (ages 6–10) is for older children to read independently or younger children to read with an adult.

The Purpose Driven Life Devotional for Kids by Rick Warren (ages 8–12) is based on the best-selling adult book.

Thank You, God! A Jewish Child's Book of Prayers by Judyth Groner and Madeline Wikler (ages 4–7) contains 21 simple prayers in Hebrew and English.

Balanced Life:

The Busy Body Book: A Kid's Guide to Fitness by Lizzy Rockwell (ages 3–7) includes information about how the body works and the importance of physical activity.

Good Enough to Eat: A Kid's Guide to Food and Nutrition by Lizzy Rockwell (ages 4–8) teaches children about the nutrient groups, digestion, and calories, and includes kid-friendly recipes.

Kid Chef: The Foodie Kids Cookbook: Healthy Recipes and Culinary Skills for the New Cook in the Kitchen by Melina Hammer (ages 8–13) is an easy-to-follow cookbook that includes sections on a variety of culinary skills for beginners in the kitchen.

Why Should I Eat Well? by Claire Llewellyn (ages 4–8) helps kids understand the importance of good eating habits.

ACTIVITIES AND GAMES

LEARNING ABOUT STRESS AND FEELINGS

Go Fish: Anchor Your Stress by Franklin Rubenstein (grades K–5) involves open-ended questions the child must answer before requesting a fish card.

Dr. Playwell's Worry-Less Game by Lawrence Shapiro (ages 6–12) features "Worry Monsters," which kids try to capture.

How Do You Doodle? Drawing My Feelings and Emotions by Elise Gravel (ages 8–12) has activities to help children express their emotions.

My Feelings Activity Book by Abbie Schiller and Samantha Kurtzman-Counter (ages 3–9) is a fill-in-the-blank activity book that helps children identify feelings and learn how to change them.

The Stress Management Game by Berthold Berg (ages 8 and up) features an anxious terrier and a cat in a board game and how they deal with common social stressors.

STRESS AT SCHOOL

How to Be a Bully . . . NOT! by Marcia Nass is a book and card game for young children that teaches what bullies do and how not to respond to it.

The Bullying Game by Berthold Berg (ages 8 and up) focuses on the victim, the bully, and the bystander, helping children understand a bully's motivation.

Stop Bullying Thumball is a 4-inch ball with 32 facets with questions or prompts about bullying.

STRESS BUSTERS

Angel Bear Yoga by Christi Eley and Mark Eley is a parent-child yoga program that includes lesson books, yoga pose playing cards, and CDs.

Breathe2Relax (older children and adults) is a stress management app with practice exercises for diaphragmatic breathing.

Guided Meditation for Primary Students by BuddhaNet includes scripts for guided meditations (available at http://www.buddhanet.net/pdf_file/med-guided2.pdf).

"Hot Air Balloon Ride: A Guided Meditation for Kids, Children's Visualization for Sleep and Dreaming" by Amelia Schmelzer is an example of one of the many children's meditations available on YouTube (available at https://www.youtube.com/watch?v=vlv6Y1tq1sQ).

Meditation Studio by Gaiam is an app, which provides meditations with special collections for kids, teens, and moms.

My Light Shines Bright (ages 8–12) is an app that features 32 guided meditations.

Sleep Meditations for Kids by Christiane Kerr (ages 4–12) is an app that features calming bedtime relaxation stories for children.

"Spider-Man: Practicing Mindfulness and Increasing Focus" by Kids Relaxation is a superhero-themed script (available at http://kidsrelaxation.com/uncategorized/spider-man-practicing-mindfulness-and-increasing-focus).

Teaching Mindfulness to Children by Karen E. Hooker and Iris E. Fodor includes an example of a guided meditation (available at http://www.gisc.org/gestaltreview/documents/teachingmindfulnesstochildren.pdf).

Yoga Pretzels by Tara Guber and Leah Kalish is a set of 50 yoga pose cards for kids and parents.

References

American Academy of Pediatrics. (2015). *AAP updates recommendations on obesity prevention: It's never too early to begin living a healthy lifestyle.* Retrieved from https://www.aap.org/en-us/about-the-aap/aap-press-room/Pages/AAP-Updates-Recommendations-on-Obesity-Prevention-It's-Never-Too-Early-to-Begin-Living-a-Healthy-Lifestyle.aspx

American Academy of Pediatrics. (2016). *American Academy of Pediatrics supports childhood sleep guidelines.* Retrieved from https://www.aap.org/en-us/about-the-aap/aap-press-room/Pages/American-Academy-of-Pediatrics-Supports-Childhood-Sleep-Guidelines.aspx

Beidas, R. S., Benjamin, C. L., Puleo, C. M., Edmunds, J. M., & Kendall, P. C. (2010). Flexible applications of the coping cat program for anxious youth. *Cognitive and Behavioral Practice, 17*, 142–153.

Berk, L. S., Fenton, D. L., Tan, S. A., Bittman, B. B., & Westengard, J. (2001). Modulation of neuroimmune parameters during the eustress of humor-associated mirthful laughter. *Alternative Therapies in Health and Medicine, 7*, 62–76.

Bernstein, B. E. (2014). Separation anxiety and school refusal. *Medscape.* Retrieved from http://emedicine.medscape.com/article/916737-overview

Brooks, R. (2015). *Continuing thoughts about resilience and caring: What we can learn from military veterans.* Retrieved from http://www.drrobertbrooks.com/continuing-thoughts-about-resilience-and-caring-what-we-can-learn-from-military-veterans

Brooks, R., & Goldstein. S. (2001). *Raising resilient children: Fostering strength, hope, and optimism in your child.* New York, NY: McGraw-Hill.

Casbarro, J. (2016). *Test anxiety: Strategies to improve student performance.* Naples, FL: National Professional Resources.

Center on the Developing Child, Harvard University. (2016). *Toxic stress.* Retrieved from http://developingchild.harvard.edu/science/key-concepts/toxic-stress

Chandler, K. (1998, January). Stressed out. *South Florida Parenting,* 62–67.

Chansky, T. E. (2014). *Freeing your child from anxiety: Powerful, practical solutions to overcome your child's fears, worries, and phobias* (Rev. ed.) New York, NY: Harmony.

Curry, N. A., & Kasser, T. (2005). Can coloring mandalas reduce anxiety? *Art Therapy, 22,* 81–85. doi:10.1080/07421656.2005.10129441

Dr. Phil. (2016). *Dr. Phil's 2 important rules when it comes to raising kids.* Retrieved from http://www.drphil.com/videos/dr-phils-2-important-rules-when-it-comes-to-raising-kids

Dweck, C. S. (2006). *Mindset: The new psychology of success.* New York, NY: Random House.

Greenspan, S. I. (2002). *The secure child: Helping our children feel safe and confident in a changing world.* Cambridge, MA: Da Capo Press.

Hooker, K., & Fodor, I. (2008). Teaching mindfulness to children. *Gestalt Review, 12*(1), 75–91.

Huberty, T. J. (2013). Anxiety and anxiety disorders in children. *Communique, 1*(8), 20–21.

Kendall, P. C., & Hedtke, K. A. (2006). *The coping cat workbook* (2nd ed.). Ardmore, PA: Workbook.

KidsHealth. (2016). *Anxiety, fears, and phobias.* Retrieved from http://kidshealth.org/en/parents/anxiety.html

Masten, A. S. & Coastworth, J. D. (1998). The development of competence in favorable and unfavorable environments: Lessons from research on successful children. *American Psychologist, 53,* 205–220.

McGonigal, K. (2013, September). *How to make stress your friend* [Video file]. Retrieved from https://www.ted.com/talks/kelly_mcgonigal_how_to_make_stress_your_friend

Miller, C. (2013). How anxiety leads to disruptive behavior: Kids who seem oppositional are often severely anxious. *Child Mind Institute.* Retrieved from http://childmind.org/article/how-anxiety-leads-to-disruptive-behavior

Mindful Schools. (2013, July 31). *A psychologist walked around a room* [Facebook update]. Retrieved from https://www.facebook.com/mindfulschools/photos/a.203073253066340.49931.165948186778847/598713920168936

Poulin, M. J., Brown, S. L., Dillard, A. J., & Smith, D. M. (2013, September). Giving to others and the association between stress and mortality. *American Journal of Public Health, 103,* 1649–1655.

Presta, R. (2016). The parents guide to teaching mindfulness to children with anxiety. *The Anxiety-Free Child Program: Advanced Strategies for Overcoming Your Child's Anxiety.* Retrieved from http://anxietyfreechild.com/mindfulness-guide

Putwain, D. (2008). Do examinations stakes moderate the test anxiety-examination performance relationship? *Educational Psychology, 28,* 109–118.

Reynolds, G. (2016, January). *To better cope with stress, listen to your body* [Web log post]. Retrieved from http://well.blogs.nytimes.com/2016/01/13/to-better-cope-with-stress-listen-to-your-body

Stock Kranowitz, C. (2016, Winter) When your child gets out-of-sync. *ADDitude: Strategies and Support for ADHD and LD,* 19–20.

Wickelgren, I. (2011). *Goldie Hawn plunges into brain science* [Web log post]. Retrieved from http://blogs.scientificamerican.com/streams-of-consciousness/goldie-hawn-plunges-into-brain-science

About the Authors

Mary Anne Richey and **James W. Forgan** have spent a combined 67 years working with children who struggle with stress-related difficulties, executive functioning deficits, and ADHD in school settings and in private practice.

Mary Anne Richey, M.Ed., is a Licensed School Psychologist in a private practice providing evaluation of children with learning differences, consultations in private and public schools, and workshops on ADHD, executive functioning difficulties, and gifted students. She also has experience as a middle school teacher, administrator, high school guidance counselor, and adjunct college instructor. In 2012, she was honored as School Psychologist of the Year by the Florida Association of School Psychologists and was a nominee for the 2013 National School Psychologist of the Year, chosen by the National Association of School Psychologists.

James W. Forgan, Ph.D., is an associate professor and Licensed School Psychologist. He teaches others how to teach and assess children with ADHD, executive functioning difficulty, and other types of learning disabilities at Florida Atlantic University. In private practice, he works with families of children with ADHD, EF, and other learning differences. Jim consults with public and private schools doing workshops on ADHD, executive functioning, dyslexia, problem solving, and accommodations for learning disabilities. You may reach him at http://jimforgan.com.

Throughout this book, Jim and Mary Anne help parents manage the issues they face and incorporate strategies to help their children succeed in school and life. They have presented at national conventions and workshops for parents and professionals on strategies for helping those with ADHD and executive functioning difficulties maximize their potential. They are coauthors of *Raising Boys With ADHD*, *Raising Girls With ADHD*, and *The Impulsive, Disorganized Child: Solutions for Parenting Kids With Executive Functioning Difficulties*. They share an integrated perspective on ADHD and executive functioning based on their experiences as parents and professionals, their academic research, and their interactions with so many other parents raising girls and boys with executive functioning difficulty and ADHD.